ALL YEAR PLANTS IN FLOWER

Vincent Gradwell Dip Hort (Hons) DMS

Contents

Introduction

For more than 14 years I have led garden tours and visits and the question most asked of me by my guests is 'What plant will grow in my garden and flower in March?' – or May, or November. So to provide the answer, I set to and recorded and logged plants that actually flower – not just produce colour through foliage or berries – during each week of the year. Of course, I had to choose which plants to include in the seasons when most plants do flower, and more of that below, but I am confident that if the reader chooses wisely from this book, his or her garden will be full of flowers all year round.

Making the plant selection

Most gardeners will have their favourite plants, some easier to grow than others. I cannot explain why some plants are my favourites, but many of them feature in this book. A number are chosen because they are easy to grow and provide a good flowering display; some have bonus qualities, such as foliage or fruits and some may have all three.

The choice of plants has been influenced by their individual qualities and the desire to create a balanced mix of perennial, long-living plants suitable for a wide range of conditions. I have not selected many trees as modern gardens are often too small to accommodate them. I've also avoided many vigorous plants as I consider them unsuitable for small gardens. Bulbs are an important component of any well-planted garden and there are many bulbous plants featured that can be slotted into the smallest of growing spaces to add colour in months when other plants in flower are few and far between.

Make space for bulbs of Eucomis 'Sparkling Burgundy', plant 105.

Gathering the data

Over a period of five years, 2007 to 2011, I have recorded the flowering time of all the main plants identified in this weekly guide. Flowering in Surrey has been compared with the flowering time in Cheshire and the plants then grouped into their respective week.

Of course plants do not flower just in the alloted week – a flowering period is usually three or four weeks. And some plants, such as *Viburnum tinus* (plant 151) and *Jasminum nudiflorum* (plant 145) will flower for many weeks. The former has been recorded as

3

flowering from October through to March or April. I have fitted them into the book when their flowers are most valuable.

Common names

When leading garden holidays and tours I always apologise to my guests when talking about plant names. I explain that I know few common names and generally talk about the scientific names. This is usually greeted with groans, however, when I ask for a common name for the shrub forsythia there is silence as very few people know this shrub as 'Golden Showers'; berberis is rarely referred to as 'Barberry' and everyone is confused with the difference between daffodil and narcissus. So please don't be daunted by the use of 'scientific' names – not only are they less prone to confusion but they are often the names you know anyway.

About the author: Vincent Gradwell

I believe my love of plants was nurtured by my time studying horticulture at RHS Wisley Gardens many years ago. Every two weeks we were required to identify 20 plants. There was always a theme to the 'ident' and in the winter the selection tested the tutor and student.

The extensive array of plants available meant that we needed to be up to date with what was in flower. This was long before digital cameras, so memory had to be relied upon. Student poverty meant that I was only able to buy two rolls of 35mm slide films during my two-year course. I have certainly made up for that over the last 45 years.

After a career with Parks and Gardens in Lancashire, I have been able to visit many gardens worldwide in my second career as an international garden tour guide. When with my groups I am often asked what is my favourite plant and where is my favourite garden and where would I choose to garden?

I love (almost) all plants, I couldn't name just one garden, and if I had to move from the UK it would probably be to an area around Elgin, northeast from Cape Town. Here is a major fruit-growing area with a lovely climate similar to southwest England but rarely, if ever, being afflicted by frost!

How to use this book

The thought behind compiling this book is that if you have a small garden there is the possibility of having at least one plant in flower each week of the year, by choosing one from each week in the book. A medium-sized garden can have two plants in flower each week and the large garden owner can have at least three plants in flower every week of the year. So, as an example, in a small garden the following plants might be chosen for January when In average winter conditions they are probably flowering throughout this four-week period:

Week 1 *Helleborus argutifolius* Week 2 *Camellia japonica*
Week 3 *Galanthus nivalis* Week 4 *Daphne odora 'Aureomarginata'*

Bulbs, climbing plants, herbaceous perennials, shrubs and a just few trees have been included, therefore by choosing carefully and thinking in 'layers', from low-lying to tree level, it is possible to maximise the use of all areas of the garden.

When garden planning, do not spread plants that flower at the same period throughout the garden as the impact may be lost. Better to group plants that will be in flower during December, January and February in the same area: it will be possible to have perhaps 15 plants in flower over at least that number of weeks, creating a real impact. Repeat the same process for other seasons.

The impact of the weather

Weather conditions can play a great part in the flowering of plants; there is reported to be a difference of eight weeks between the first flowering of daffodils in Land's End and those in John o' Groats. However with certain, particularly endemic, plants the difference is never so diverse.

The severe winters of 2009/10 and 2010/11 affected the flowering of plants greatly, but after 2009/10 all the early flowering plants seemed to flower better than following a mild winter. Bad winters also seem to lessen the difference between different parts of the country. The years during which I have recorded and photographed the plants for this book have shown some variations between Surrey and Cheshire but in the final year of checking (2011) in the majority of cases there was perhaps only one or two weeks difference between the weeks stated.

Grouped plants: top: Plant 11 Daphne odora 'Aureomarginata', middle Plant 24 Helleborus x hybridus, bottom Plant 22 Narcissus 'Tete a Tete'.

Lack of rain or drought can curtail flowering of certain plants and can even prevent the onset of flowering. As we live in a country with unpredictable weather we have come to accept that anything is possible.

Although I am not a botanist, I believe that day length probably asserts as much influence as temperature on the start of flowering. Even though the weather can be cold and frosty, as the days lengthen plants still start to flower despite a temperature drop.

The succession of flowering is the key to having plants in flower every week. I have checked periodically with friends and relatives in Scotland and various parts of England to see what is flowering at particular weeks of the year but obviously there is no guarantee that clones of the same plant will flower to order. No matter where you reside in the United Kingdom, the order of flowering will be continuous following the numbered weeks in the book. Enjoy your flowers!

Glossary

If you encounter unusual words in the plant descriptions, here is an explanation.

Acid describes the soil type measured on a ph scale where ph7 is neutral, less than this is acid, greater than ph7 is alkaline.

Alternate leaves which are spaced along a stem at opposite sides to each other, one at each node.

Anther the upper part of a stamen, usually containing the pollen.

Axil the angle formed between the leaf petiole and stem, usually the location of a bud.

Axillary pertaining to a bud or flower growing in the leaf axil.

Bipinnate a compound leaf in which the leaflets are also pinnately divided.

Bract or **Bracteole** a modified leaf, usually at the base of a flower or flowerhead.

Calcareous describing a soil which is alkaline, with a high proportion of calcium carbonate, e.g. chalk.

Calyx a group of modified leaves, 'sepals', which often enclose the flower parts, sometimes persisting on to fruit production e.g. tomato.

Capsid a sap-sucking insect pest, often causing severe damage to buds and flowers.

Clone a selection of plants all identical to its parent generally propagated vegetatively.

Corm an underground swollen organ, for storage of starch to withstand a period of dormancy.

Corolla usually the colourful parts of a flower; generally used for petals fused together to form a tube.

Corymb a flat-topped inflorescence.

Cultivar shortened form of 'cultivated variety' usually developed by man's selection or hybridisation.

Cyathia [plural: **cyathium**] specialised floral parts only found in Euphorbia species, consisting of a single female flower and several male flowers.

Cyme a branched inflorescence with a round or flat shape, each branch ending with a flower.

Dioecious having male and female flowers on separate plants.

Disc floret usually small simple flowers, generally tubular, forming the central disc of a flowerhead, eg *Asteraceae*.

Elliptic a leaf shape, broadest at the centre tapering at either end.

Entire smooth and without lobes or toothed margins.

Ericaceous of the family *Ericaceae*, including Erica and Calluna.

Fall petal the drooping or pendent tepal of an Iris flower.

Farina white or mealy, looking as covered with flour.

Forma (f) variant of a species, naturally occurring with minor variations not sufficiently different to be classed as a separate species or variety.

Garden origin not naturally occurring, usually modified or hybridised by man.

Genus the primary category of plant name, between family and specific name.

Glaucous usually describes leaves or stems, with a white or blue grey bloom.

Hermaphrodite flowers with both male and female flower parts.

Indumentum usually found on the underside of leaves, consisting of fine hairs or scales.

Internode a section of stem between two nodes.

Labiate a plant belonging to the family *Labiatae*.

Midrib usually the main or central vein of a leaf, from the stalk to the leaf tip.

Modified leaf leaves altered by nature to resemble other plant parts.

Monoecious separate male and female flowers but appearing on the same plant.

Node the point on a stem which contains a leaf or several and axillary buds.

Opposite pairs of leaves at each node but on opposite sides.

Ovary female organ of a flower in which can be found the ovules or seeds.

Ovate egg shaped, where the widest point is below the middle.

Palmate a compound leaf divided into leaflets arising from a central point or a leaf lobed and shaped like a hand.

Panicle a branched raceme of flowers.

Perfoliate applied to leaves without stalks, united at the base and clasping the stem.

Perianth an inclusive term for the corolla and the calyx.

Petaloid looking like a petal in shape and colour.

Petiole the leaf stalk, joining the leaf blade to the plant stem.

Pinnate a compound leaf, composed of several leaflets, often arranged in opposite pairs.

Raceme an inflorescence consisting of flowers on stalks, the youngest flower being towards the top.

Ray floret small simple flower, usually forming the colourful outer parts of a flower head eg *Asteraceae*.

Recurved lobe arched backwards.

Reflexed bent sharply backwards.

Remontant a plant that flowers more than once in a growing season.

Rhizome horizontal fleshy underground stem or sometimes on the surface, by which a plant spreads.

Salverform a tubular flower that flattens out to horizontal lobes.

Sepal one segment of the calyx, usually green but can be petal like, *see* tepal.

Species (sp) category of plant nomenclature, identifying plants which are identical, and breed true from seed.

Stamen the male part of a flower, consisting of an anther usually supported on a filament.

Stellate star-shaped, with pointed petals.

Sterile flower a part on an inflorescence, looking like a flower, but without the reproductive parts.

Stigma or **Style** the central part of a flower which receives pollen, connecting to the ovary.

Stolon a creeping stem at or below ground level producing roots at the nodes and shoots at its tip.

Tepal sepal modified to resemble colourful petals.

Toothed describing the margin or edge of a leaf which has triangular indentations.

Tripartite divided into three more or less equal lobes.

Umbel an inflorescence of numerous stalked flowers, generally forming a flat top, with flower stalks of different lengths.

MID
WINTER

The most challenging season for flowers, but a challenge that can be overcome with a clever plant selection.

Weeks 1-9

The winter months may be considered to be the most depressing time in most gardens, but of course this need not be the case. There are hundreds of plants that are at their best in the coolest time of the year. The low temperatures also have the advantage of increasing the flowering period of many plants. In the hot summer season, many hardy plants flower over a period of two to three weeks. However in the winter and early spring many will continue to flower for six weeks or more.

Here a swathe of Cyclamen coum (plant 4) has been planted beneath a tree, the nodding heads above a carpet of variegated leaves providing a bank of colour for weeks on end in the early months of the year.

Chimonanthus praecox

Family: Calycanthaceae Common name: Wintersweet

Originating from China and Japan, the plant was discovered by plant collectors and introduced into the United Kingdom around 1766. It was first grown under glass for protection.

This highly scented shrub produces its very heady spicy aroma from delicate flowers in the middle of winter's worst weather. Even when it cannot be seen there will no doubt of its presence in the cold winter breeze.

This is a deciduous shrub growing to a height of 3m (10ft) and having a spread of 2m (6ft). Large light-green leaves are produced in well-spaced pairs along the branches. Leaves are lance-shaped and approximately 15–20cm (6–8in) long and 8–10cm (3–4in) wide; they turn yellow in the autumn. Flowers are delicate, having almost translucent petals in clusters of three or five. Each flower is bowl-shaped with many pale straw coloured petals, approximately 2cm (1in) across, while the inner petals are marked with crimson.

Preferring an acid soil, the plant will tolerate shade or a sunny position. Plant close to a door or gate, or adjacent to a path or driveway, so that the plant's best feature, its scent, can be appreciated by all.

Varieties & Forms

CHIMONANTHUS PRAECOX 'GRANDIFLORUS' (AGM)
Has deep-yellow flowers up to 3.5cm (1½in) across. The largest of any of the forms available. Inner petals are striped with maroon.

CHIMONANTHUS PRAECOX 'LUTEUS' AGM Pure-yellow flowers that open widely.

CHIMONANTHUS PRAECOX 'PARVIFLORUS' Flowers are pale yellow to lemon yellow with no markings on the petals.

Helleborus argutifolius AGM
Family: Ranunculaceae Common name: Winter Hellebore

Its earlier name was *H. corsicus*, which gave a clue to its wild origins, being found on both Corsica and Sardinia. Usually flowers in January but may be in bud for several weeks before.

Growing to a height of 75cm (30in) the stems carry sharply pointed and toothed leaves, dark green above and silvery beneath, and consisting of three leaflets; each up to 8cm (3in) long and borne on long leaf stalks. Flowers are produced as terminal cymes (flat-topped clusters) on previous year's growth. There may be 20 or more greenish bowl-shaped flowers 3–5cm (1–2in) across with a prominent cluster of greenish-yellow stamens.

Seeds are produced readily and seedlings may become a nuisance in certain conditions. Old flowered stems collapse untidily and turn woody. Leaves blacken during the summer as the new stems are produced.

Plants prefer a neutral or slightly alkaline soil, fertile and humus-rich, in either light shade or full sun. Cut down old flowered stems as soon as new stems are a few centimetres high. Top dress annually with well-rotted garden compost or leaf mould.

Varieties & Forms

HELLEBORUS FOETIDUS Green flowers, sometimes with a light fragrance; petals often with purple margins.

11

Hamamelis mollis

Family: Hamamelidaceae Common name: Chinese Witch Hazel

Originally collected by George Wilson but introduced in 1879 from south-eastern China.

This beautifully scented flowering shrub is a delight to two senses, sight and smell. Its almond fragrance blown about in the cold winter air can often be smelled long before the shrub is in view. Flowering sometimes commences in December, but more usually January and February.

Clusters of tiny petals, crimped as though they have been tightly folded, are produced before the foliage and although they are normally a bright golden yellow, there are many other forms and colours. These include pale lemon yellow, orange and some almost red. Leaves are up to 10cm (4in) across, large, hairy and deeply veined, and follow the flowers in April. Leaf stalks may also be 10cm (4in) long. The dark-green leaves turn yellow or orange in the autumn before they fall.

Slow-growing, this shrub is suitable for a shaded or sunny position, although if sunny there may be a risk of some frost damage to the delicate petals.

Varieties & Forms

HAMAMELIS x 'JELENA' AGM
A very vigorous form raised in Belgium, named after the wife of the plant breeder. Flowers are very dark pink.

HAMAMELIS VERNALIS 'SANDRA' AGM Has red flowers, dark young foliage with good autumn colour.

Cyclamen coum

Family: Primulaceae Common name: Sowbread

One of several species of cyclamen that are hardy in the United Kingdom. It can be found growing in the wild in Eastern Europe, including Bulgaria, Turkey and Lebanon. It is the earliest cyclamen to flower; buds can often be seen in late December.

a slight fragrance. After flowering the plant produces a seed capsule containing up to 20 irregular-shaped seeds. The seed stalk then coils to bring the seed capsule closer to the soil surface.

Plants grow from underground tubers, which are dark-brown or black, flattened and up to 15cm (6in) across. Cyclamen should not be allowed to dry out completely or they will often fail to commence into growth. New plants can be raised from freshly harvested seed.

Usually the pink, white or red flowers are produced in January and February, sometimes even into March. Leaves are round or kidney-shaped approximately 3–6cm (1–3in) across; although up to 10cm (4in) long leaf stalks lie along the ground and so only appear to be 4–5cm (1½–2in) high. These are produced during the autumn and remain until around June or early July. Leaves are dark-green or mottled silver, generally with a dark-red underside.

Flowers are small with reflexed petals; often the mouth is marked with a darker colour than the petals. Sometimes the flowers have

Varieties & Forms

CYCLAMEN COUM Subsp. CAUCASICUM Has lilac-pink flowers and heart-shaped leaves with silver markings.

CYCLAMEN COUM F. ALBISSIMUM This form has white flowers with red markings around the mouth.

CYCLAMEN PEWTER GROUP AGM Variable leaves, as they are raised from seed; there are many types, some with more silver marking than others.

13

Camellia japonica
Family: Theaceae

China, northern India and the Himalayas are the home of the camellia, however the majority of plants seen in garden centres and private gardens are hybrids. There has been a great deal of activity by plant breeders and there are now several hundred varieties of *C. japonica* and *C. x Williamsii*. It is the same genus of plants from which are gathered leaves to make tea. Leaves of *C. sinensis* are picked to make both green and black tea.

The variety shown to the left, *C.* 'Mary Costa', has large, anemone-form white flowers up to 7cm (3in) across.

Camellias can only be grown successfully in acid soils; any with lime or chalk will result in poor growth and chlorosis (yellowing) of the leaves. A moisture-retentive soil with plenty of organic matter is required, and position camellias in a lightly shaded place to ensure that early-morning sun will not damage the flowers that open in frosty months of the year. Pruning is only required to remove dead or diseased wood and thereby retain the health and shape of the shrub.

Camellia japonica is a slow-growing evergreen shrub attaining a height of 4m (13ft); leaves are thick and leathery, dark-green and 7–10cm (3–4in) long. Its habit is generally upright but often the weight of the flowers will bend the branches to make the shrub appear more spreading. There are several hundreds of hybrids and cultivars and flowers are either single, double or anemone-flowered, and in red, pink or white.

C. japonica has been selected as a suitable alternative, being more hardy, to Plant 5A but the camellia may also suffer frost damage to the delicate flowers.

Acacia dealbata AGM

Family: Mimosaceae
(Leguminosae)
Common name: Silver Wattle

Large shrub or small tree from Australia, found growing in the wild in New South Wales and Victoria. It is sometimes called mimosa as this is the acacia commonly sold by florists in the United Kingdom.

There are numerous members of the mimosa family but only some are hardy in the United Kingdom. The Silver Wattle is one of the hardiest and will survive in all but the coldest and most exposed counties. The specific name *dealbata* means 'whitened' and refers to the silvery underside of the leaves.

Flower buds appear during November or December and it only takes a few mild days in January or February for the buds to burst into a profusion of pale yellow pompoms. Flowers are approximately 6mm (½in) across and in densely crowded terminal racemes up to 25cm (10in) long. Its delicate almond-scented fragrance is obvious in sunny conditions.

Leaves are like tiny fern fronds; each leaflet is about 2mm long with up to 60 leaflets per leaf with silvery undersides. The twigs and bark remain green for many years but will eventually change to brown. Generally attaining a height of 6–15m (20–48ft), it only achieves its maximum size in well-sheltered positions. In frost-prone areas train against a wall; prune to keep within its allocated place, but not too severely as acacia often refuse to produce new shoots from older wood.

Varieties & Forms

ACACIA ARABICA Grown in North Africa; produces gum arabic.

ACACIA PRAVISSMA Very different in appearance, having triangular leaves and numerous pendulous racemes of bright-yellow flowers in March and April.

15

Erica lusitanica AGM

Family: Ericaceae Common name: Portuguese Heath

Found growing in the wild in Southern Europe including Spain, France and Portugal. In its natural habitat it will attain a height of approximately 3.5m (11ft), but the selections usually available for planting in the United Kingdom grow to a height of around 2m (6ft).

A stiff upright-growing plant with numerous main stems. Leaves are dark green, up to 7mm (¼in) long in whorls of three or four around the thin stems. Small pointed flowers approximately 6mm (¼in) long are produced in long axillary racemes. Flowers often have pink markings around the mouth. Flowering can commence in December and will continue until March, except in extreme weather. Requires an acid soil in a sheltered position to provide protection from cold winds.

Varieties & Forms

ERICA LUSITANICA 'GEORGE HUNT' Has yellowish green leaves, but needs to be sheltered from cold winds avoiding exposed sites.

ERICA AUSTRALIS Flowering in spring, up to 2m (6ft). Its larger pink flowers grow up to 9mm (½in) long.

Crocus tommasinianus AGM
Family: Iridaceae

Most crocus originate from the Mediterranean countries including Greece, Turkey, Hungary, the Balkans and parts of Asia, where it favours woodlands and calcareous (chalky) soils. *C. tommasinianus* is one of the earliest crocus to flower in the United Kingdom.

Flowers are variable, pale-lilac outside the flower with darker purple inside. Some are almost white; however, the long slender tube is always white, being produced at the same time as small basal leaves from small corms. Flowers grow to a height of 10–15cm (4–6in) but leaves extend to around 20cm (8in) after flowering is complete. Leaves are narrow, about 5mm (¼in) wide with a conspicuous whitish mid rib. The corms produce numerous offsets and so clumps rapidly spread. Seeds are also freely produced so that in undisturbed areas rapid colonisation occurs. After a number of years it is wise to split up the clumps to prevent overcrowding.

Varieties & Forms

CROCUS TOMMASINIANUS f. 'ALBUS' Produces all-white flowers having no other colour at all.

CROCUS TOMMASINIANUS 'WHITEWELL PURPLE' Rapidly produces large clumps, having purple/red flowers, pale-mauve inside.

CROCUS TOMMASINIANUS 'RUBY GIANT' Larger sterile flowers of a darker purple colour.

Vinca major

Family: Apocynaceae **Common name: Greater Periwinkle**

Grows wild in several European countries, including in the Mediterranean region. All parts of the plant may cause stomach upsets if ingested.

A creeping shrublet, often scrambling through other plants and may become invasive. The cultivar 'Variegata' is less vigorous and has fewer flowers; this may not be important, as this plant's main attraction is its variegated foliage. Spasmodic blue salverform flowers, 2–4cm (1–1½in) across are produced during the winter and spring. More flowers are produced when grown in sunny positions. Dark-green leaves, produced in opposite pairs rounded or more or less elliptical, are approximately 3–5cm (1–2in) long on spreading arching stems, which root on contact with the soil surface. In dry seasons the plant is susceptible to rust disease.

Varieties & Forms

VINCA MAJOR 'VARIEGATA' AGM
Leaves have cream margins.

VINCA MAJOR 'MACULATA' Pale greenish-yellow leaves with darker margins.

VINCA MAJOR Var. 'OXYLOBA'
With dark-purple, star-shaped flowers with distinctly pointed petals.

Galanthus nivalis AGM

Family: Amaryllidaceae Common name: Snowdrop

Snowdrops are thought of as a plant following snow and thereby heralding spring. But in fact, if current winters are anything to go by, snowdrops often start to flower before any snow falls. Often seen to best advantage in large naturalised drifts, they appear to do well in churchyards. The common snowdrop *G. nivalis* may appear to be a British wild plant due to its ability to seed and multiply quickly, however, it originates from mainland Europe, ranging from France across to Russia.

Flowers are produced during the winter months just before the leaves develop. Flowers are variable, consisting of three outer tepals and three inner tepals, notched and marked with green. The flowers open almost as soon as they emerge from the soil and continue to expand as the flower stalk extends to carry the flowers clear of the foliage, which can be as high as 18cm (7in). Leaves are bluish green and up to 15cm (6in) high. In dry conditions flowering is brief and the foliage dies down very quickly. Does best in organically rich soil, moist but freely draining, and in light shade.

Growing from small bulbs, these are best planted whilst still in leaf so that the bulbs do not dry out. When naturalised in grass or in very shady conditions, snowdrops may not commence flowering until February, but on occasions they can be found in flower in December.

Varieties & Forms

GALANTHUS ELWESII AGM
Has bluish glaucous foliage.

GALANTHUS 'ATKINSII' AGM Taller than many species, may reach 30cm (12in).

GALANTHUS 'JOHN GRAY' Flowers may attain a size of 4cm (1½in) across. Named after a gardener from Suffolk.

Leucojum vernum AGM
Family: Amaryllidaceae Common name: Spring Snowflake

Although the scientific name and common name indicate this bulbous plant flowers in spring, in most years flowering commences in winter and I have recorded it flowering in early January in Cumbria. A native of southern Europe, growing in sheltered areas on mountains, bulbs naturalise well under deciduous trees or on woodland edges.

As soon as the flowers emerge above the soil surface they are open, white bells with greenish-yellow markings on each petal, approximately 3cm (1½in) across. Stems will ultimately grow to 30cm (12in) high. Bulbs each produce a cluster of dark-green, narrow and erect leaves approximately 20–25cm (8–10in) long. Plant in early autumn in fertile humus-rich soil so that bulbs do not dry out.

Narcissus flies may be a problem as they lay eggs amongst the dying foliage; the grubs hatch and move to the bulbs where they eat the centre. Remove foliage as soon as it has died down and then mulch the soil surface to hide the necks of the bulbs.

Varieties & Forms

LEUCOJUM VERNUM Var. CARPATHICUM Has white flowers with yellow markings.

LEUCOJUM VERNUM Var. VAGNERI A vigorous form with two flowers per stem.

Daphne odora 'Aureomarginata'
Family: Thymelaeaceae

The variegated form of *D. odora* is hardier than the species, although in most winters both do well in many areas of the United Kingdom, apart from very exposed areas. Originating from China and Japan, this shrub has been cultivated for many years.

This slow-growing shrub will eventually attain a height of 1.5m (5ft) with a congested branching habit. Evergreen, except in harsh winters, leaves are lance-shaped, dark-green and with creamy-white margins, up to 7cm (3in) long. Clusters of deep-pink star-shaped flowers are approximately 1cm (½in) across with a paler inside and are produced towards the tip of the new growth or occasionally lower down. Flowers are very fragrant and red fruits are formed following flowering. Fruits and most parts of this plant are poisonous and some people are sensitive even to exposure to the plant's sap.

Preferring well-draining soil, the plant does not take kindly to dry soils; it is advisable to mulch annually with well-rotted garden compost or other organic material. *D. odora* will tolerate some light shade but a sunny position is best.

Varieties & Forms

DAPHNE ODORA Of similar habit but less hardy and with no variegated leaf margins.

DAPHNE ODORA f. ALBA Has white flowers.

DAPHNE BHOLUA 'JACQUELINE POSTILL' AGM Fully hardy and having larger flowers and a stronger fragrance.

Sarcoccoca confusa AGM

Family: Buxaceae Common name: Sweet Box

An evergreen shrub with dark-green glossy foliage and very fragrant flowers; from China and other Asian countries, where it grows in shady thickets and woodlands.

A low-growing evergreen shrub with dark-green, glossy, pointed leaves up to 6cm (2½in) long. In winter and early spring clusters of small white flowers appear over several weeks – whitish clusters of stamens are produced without petals but with a very strong fragrance. Separate male and female flowers are both found in these clusters in the leaf axils and are followed by round, shiny, black fruits 5mm (¼in) across.

The shrub will tolerate dry shady situations or woodland edges and can grow up to 2m (6ft) with a spread of 1m (3ft) but can be trimmed to restrict the height. It can also be used as an informal hedge as it is slow growing and tolerates a wide variety of positions. Plant close to house windows, garden paths or the patio so that the heady scent can be appreciated in winter.

Varieties & Forms

SARCOCOCA HOOKERIANA Var. DIGYNA 'PURPLE STEM' AGM
Forms a thicket of stems reddish in colour; flowers have a pink tinge.

SARCOCOCA HUMILIS Grows up to 1m (3ft), leaves are narrow and pointed. Flowers are tinged with pink.

Erica erigena

Family: Ericaceae **Common name: Irish Heath**

An upright evergreen shrub found in the wild in Europe, including Spain, Portugal and Ireland. It was formerly known as *Erica mediterranea*. This photograph of *E. erigena* 'Brian Proudley' (right) was taken in January at RHS Wisley Gardens in Surrey.

Leaves are small and narrow, typical of heaths (Erica),about 1cm (½in) long. Having a lengthy flowering period, continuing through to March or April, dark-pink or white flowers are produced in profusion up to 5mm (¼in) long. The flowers are sweetly scented and the plant can grow to a height of 2m (6ft) and spread to approximately 90cm (3ft). This plant requires a well-draining acid soil to grow successfully.

Brittle stems can be damaged in exposed situations, so provide some shelter. Lightly trim after flowering in the spring, removing flowered stems and any dead wood to retain a compact bushy shape.

Varieties & Forms

ERICA ERIGENA 'BRIGHTNESS'
Has foliage that turns purplish during the winter months and lilac-pink flowers in April and May.

ERICA ERIGENA 'GOLDEN LADY'
AGM Yellowish-green foliage; compact, only growing to 40cm (16in).

ERICA ERIGENA 'SUPERBA' Pale-pink strongly scented flowers are produced on very vigorous plants up to 2m (6ft). Good as a hedging plant.

Eranthis hyemalis AGM

Family: Ranunculaceae Common name: Winter Aconite

Grows wild in Europe, including the South of France, Italy, Austria and Bulgaria. Quickly multiplies to form clumps with small blackish tubers.

Shoots appear in late winter as a welcome golden-yellow flower bud with a ruff of bright-green leaves. Flowers open to be cup-shaped approximately 3cm (1¼in) across having six bright-yellow petal-like sepals and a central cluster of yellow stamens; slowly develop to a height of 5–8cm (2–3in). The ruff of leaves that surround the stem are only 2–3cm (about 1in) long and appear like green fingers, perfectly showing off the delicate yellow flowers. As the petals drop the stem continues to grow to 15cm (6in) and produces tripartite (three-part) seed capsules, each part with a distinct hooked point. Additional basal leaves, palmate-shaped and 2–4cm (1–1½in) long, may also develop.

In the garden this plant can be successfully naturalised in grass under deciduous trees where it will rapidly produce plant colonies. Its preference is a position in light dappled shade or full sun.

Congested clumps may be divided after flowering, but replant immediately as the tubers do not like to dry out; plant in fertile soil with adequate humus to retain soil moisture. Because of these requirements slugs and snails may be a problem.

Varieties & Forms

ERANTHIS CILICIA Has slightly larger flowers.

ERANTHIS TUBERGENII 'GUINEA GOLD' AGM A hybrid between E. hyemalis and E. cilicia.

ERANTHIS PINNATIFIDA Produces white flowers; grows wild in Japan.

Garrya elliptica

Family: Garryaceae Common name: Silk Tassel Bush

Originally from the western areas of the USA where it grows in woodlands, but also found in countries of Central America and the Caribbean.

Upright-growing large shrub up to 4m (13ft) high. Ovate dark-green wavy-edged leaves up to 7.5cm (3in) long have paler undersides. Flowers are produced in catkins; the longest catkins are composed of male flowers, as much pollen is required for wind pollination. Dependent upon the clone (propagation of new plants from a parent selected for long catkins), catkins can be 14–22cm (5–9in) long. The male catkins are greyish with protruding yellow stamens from which large quantities of pollen are produced.

Grow in a position with some shelter from cold drying winter winds, and against a wall in cold areas is best. Cold winds can cause unsightly leaf damage, which will persist until new leaves are produced in late spring. A fertile well-draining soil is needed for best results. Minimal pruning is required. When buying new plants, make the selection when in flower so that a male plant can be chosen.

Varieties & Forms

GARRYA ELLIPTICA 'EVIE' Often has catkins longer than 30cm (12in).

GARRYA ELLIPTICA 'JAMES ROOF' AGM Produces large numbers of catkins approximately 20cm (8in) long and has dark-green leaves.

Iris 'Katharine Hodgkin'
Family Iridaceae

This low-growing bulbous iris of the *I.reticulata* style is of garden origin, but the parent species were first found in the Caucasus Mountains and Turkey.

Flowering in late winter, the bulbs produce pointed sheathed flower buds, which in mild weather split to reveal beautifully marked flowers, pale-blue with yellow, white and violet-blue markings. At flowering time the flowers are approximately 12cm (5in) high and 8cm (3in) across. The flowers are short-lived unless the weather is mild and calm. Two or three square sectioned leaves follow after the flowers fade and grow to a height of 30cm (12in), then disappear after a short time.

The bulbs are susceptible to fungal diseases and therefore require well-draining soil in full sun or light shade. Slugs and snails find the flowers very appetising, so spread sharp stones or coarse grit among the emerging flowers.

Varieties & Forms

IRIS 'JOYCE' This iris has pale-blue flowers with dark-blue and yellow markings on the falls.

IRIS 'NATASCHA' With graceful very pale blue, almost white flowers.

Erica carnea 'C.J. Backhouse'

Family: Ericaceae Common name: Winter Heath

One of the best *E. carnea* varieties, flowering over a long period, often for up to ten weeks during the winter months.

Dark-pink, almost red, flowers commence opening in December and often there are still flowers on the plant in March. Grows to a height of approximately 45cm (18in). This plant is best clipped over with a pair of shears immediately after flowering in March or April to remove all flowered stems and to prevent the plant from becoming leggy.

Ensure the removal of all prunings to prevent fungal diseases, which can cause defoliation and the death of parts of the plant. For a detailed description of the plant characteristics see *Erica* 'Springwood White' (plant 19).

Varieties & Forms

ERICA CARNEA 'KING GEORGE'
Dark pink flowers, one of the earliest to commence flowering.

ERICA CARNEA 'FOXHOLLOW'
Masses of pink flowers on low plants, with yellow/orange new foliage.

Rosmarinus officinalis

Family: Labiatae Common name: Rosemary

Originating from the Mediterranean countries of Europe and the Middle East, this plant prefers a well-draining soil. It revels in warm sunshine as shady conditions inhibit flowering and reduce the aromatic oils within the plant. Frost damage may occur in very hard winters.

to 5cm (2in) long with a grey-silver underside, and grow in pairs with obvious axillary buds. This shrub will grow up to 2m (6ft) tall in good conditions and can have a similar spread.

Grow in well-draining soil; often the poorest soils produce the best flowering. Sometimes shrubs suffer from lower branches dying back, but do not prune into older wood as new growth will not occur. May also be grown as a hedge; it should be trimmed immediately after flowering in early spring.

Varieties & Forms

ROSMARINUS OFFICINALIS 'PROSTRATUS' AGM Only grows to 20cm (8in) and the least hardy of any variety.

ROSMARINUS OFFICINALIS 'BENENDEN BLUE' This variety has rich blue flowers.

ROSMARINUS OFFICINALIS 'MISS JESSOP'S UPRIGHT' AGM Very vigorous, upright and free flowering.

An evergreen shrub that becomes leggy and untidy if not pruned; the brittle nature of the branches can result in wind damage.

Flowers are pale blue with a darker blue lower lip approximately 2cm (1in) long. They are produced from February to May and sometimes again in the autumn. Leaves are thick and leathery, up

Erica carnea 'Springwood White' AGM

Family: Ericaceae **Common name: Winter Heath**

This is only one of the winter heaths, of which there are hundreds of varieties. They all flower during the winter and early spring months, bringing a welcome mound of white, pink or red flowers. *E. carnea* originates from Europe and in particular northwest Italy, the Balkans and other eastern European countries.

The plant is low and spreading, growing 15–25cm (6–10in) high and spreading up to 75cm (30in) across. It is evergreen and produces small mid-green linear leaves 5–10mm (¼-½in) long with curled or rolled leaf margins. Urn-shaped white flowers are borne in one-sided racemes with prominent brown anthers. Flowers are 5–10mm (¼-½in) long and are long lasting in winter temperatures.

Planting a range of varieties can result in a colourful display over many weeks. They prefer a well-drained acid soil in full sun. However, as it is not always possible to provide optimal growing sites, they will tolerate less favourable conditions. Although the soil should drain freely, mulch regularly with organic material such as garden compost.

When flowering is finished trim back using shears to remove all the flowering stems and encourage new shoots from low down, so keeping the plant neat and compact. Ensure that all clippings are removed from the plant.

Varieties & Forms

ERICA 'FOXHOLLOW' AGM Golden-yellow foliage bronzing in cold winters; flowers shell-pink in late winter to spring.

ERICA 'NATHALIE' Large deep-pink flowers on neat mound-forming plants (pictured below).

Bergenia 'Silberlicht AGM'

Family: Saxifragaceae Common name: Elephant's Ears

This is a very early flowering hybrid developed over many years. The common bergenia species are *B. crassifolia* and *B. cordifolia*, which grow wild in Siberia. There are other species from central Europe and Asia, including the Himalayas.

The origins of these species indicate how rugged and hardy these plants are, capable of withstanding harsh conditions. However, some of the modern hybrids are not as tough.

They are all clump-forming, evergreen, perennial plants with large green leaves ovate or obovate in shape about 15–25cm (6–10in) across. Some show red tinges in the leaves during the winter, which can add to the interest of these plants that are useful in difficult areas of ground covering.

B. 'Silberlicht' has white tubular flowers produced in panicles on stems up to 40cm (16in) high in early spring. Slowly changing to pink, the floral display is further enhanced by the long-lasting dark pink sepals.

Grow in humus-rich, but well-draining soil in sun or partial shade. Dense shade will reduce flowering and very hot dry conditions are not tolerated. Caterpillars may eat the foliage and vine weevils may be a problem, as they feed on the creeping stems and roots.

Varieties & Forms

BERGENIA 'BALLAWLEY' Has bronzed foliage in winter, red stems 45–60cm (18-24in) with crimson, red flowers in late spring.

BERGENIA CILIATA With large, mid-green, hairy leaves and pink-and-white flowers. In frosty weather this species may lose its foliage.

BERGENIA PURPURASCENS AGM Has green leaves with purple undersides. Reddish-purple flowers on stems up to 45cm (18in) in late spring. Foliage turns red-bronze in the winter months.

Rhododendron dauricum
Family: Ericaceae

This popular shrub originates from Hokkaido, Japan, northern China and even eastern Siberia. It flourishes in dry woodlands in mountainous areas, flowering in April and May.

Slow growing, *R. dauricum* will eventually attain a height of 2.5m (8ft). Clusters of pinkish-purple flowers up to 2cm (1in) long are produced at the end of February and into March. Flowers have prominent styles and stamens, extending beyond the flower tube. Leaves are small and leathery, often sparsely distributed over the branches, making the shrub's appearance a little untidy.

As with most rhododendrons, an acid soil is favoured, but neutral soil is accepted. Top dress regularly with well-rotted garden compost or leaf mould to provide a humus-rich soil. In severe wintry weather it will become almost deciduous.

Varieties & Forms

RHODODENDRON 'PRAECOX'
AGM A hybrid with R. dauricum as a parent is similar, best grown in semi-shade to prevent frost damaging the flowers. Will succeed in a neutral soil.

Narcissus 'Tête-à-tête' AGM
Family: Amaryllidaceae

One of the earliest narcissus to appear, usually flowering in mid to late February. Raised in Cornwall in 1949, 'Tête-à-tête' results from the crossing of *N. cyclamineus* with *N. tazetta*.

Narrow bright-green leaves up to 20cm (8in) high are produced early in the year. Flowering stems may bear up to three bright-yellow flowers 6–7cm (2–2½in) across. The perianth (outer whorl) segments are slightly reflexed and the small cup is a darker yellow.

A vigorous plant that multiplies quickly and requires regular dividing, grow in moist but free-draining soil in full sun or light shade. Slugs and snails may damage emerging flowers and bulbs may be damaged or killed by narcissus flies. Remove any dying foliage immediately to prevent the narcissus flies from being attracted to the plant.

Narcissus are grouped into 12 divisions according to their characteristics and this variety is in division 12. Some others in this division are listed under Varieties.

Varieties & Forms

NARCISSUS 'JUMBLIE' Clusters of small, nodding, bright-yellow flowers, with sharply reflexed perianth segments.

NARCISSUS 'QUINCE' This variety has several short stems per bulb; up to three pale-yellow flowers on each stem.

Forsythia x intermedia 'Spectabilis'

Family: Oleaceae Common name: Golden Shower

Described as being of garden origin, 'Spectabilis' was raised from seed in Germany in 1885 and is probably the most widely planted forsythia in the United Kingdom. It is believed to have F. suspensa and F. viridissima as its parents and is one of several varieties commonly available.

Flowers in clusters of two or three are bright yellow, approximately 2cm (1in) across with five or six corolla lobes. One of the main distinguishing features for forsythia identification is style length. *F. x intermedia* 'Spectabilis' has short styles.

It is fast growing, often producing vigorous shoots up to 1.5m (5ft) in a season following pruning. Young stems are yellowish green with corky spots or ribs and soft pithy centres. Let unpruned, the shrub can grow to 3m (10ft).

Flowers are produced in March or early April on bare stems followed by lance-shaped, bright-green leaves oppositely arranged and up to 10cm (4in) long.

Prune after flowering is over to first remove dead, dying or older flowering stems; try to retain a balance of older and newer stems. Birds can be a pest by eating the flower buds just as the flowers begin to emerge.

Varieties & Forms

FORSYTHIA 'ARNOLD DWARF'
A low-growing spreading shrub with small leaves and greenish-yellow flowers.

FORSYTHIA OVATA Only growing to 1.5m (5ft) and originating from Korea, has short-petalled flowers.

FORSYTHIA x INTERMEDIA 'ARNOLD GIANT' Fewer but larger flowers over a long flowering period.

Helleborus x hybridus
Family: Ranunculaceae Common name: Lenten Rose

Sometimes identified as *Helleborus orientalis*, but much hybridisation has been undertaken both naturally and deliberately by plant breeders.

Dark-green deeply divided palmate leaves over winter until flowering, after which new foliage is produced. Leaflets are toothed and up to 10cm (4in) on petioles that are up to 25cm (10in) long, often lying on the soil surface.

Flowers of unnamed seedlings are variable and sometimes appear as early as November in mild weather, depending on the selection grown. A wide colour spectrum is available from green to cream, white and yellow through to pink and dark purple. Generally flowers are bowl-shaped, 3–7cm (1½–3in) across.

Numerous named hybrids have been produced and self seeding is very common. Unnamed seedlings can be very competitively priced.

Plants spread from a thick, fleshy, underground rhizome and flourish in dappled shady conditions in a moisture-retentive soil.

Varieties & Forms

HELLEBORUS x HYBRIDUS 'CITRON' Pale-yellow bowl-shaped flowers.

HELLEBORUS x HYBRIDUS 'PLUTO' Small, dark, reddish-purple flowers with green flecks and stripes.

HELLEBORUS x HYBRIDUS 'COSMOS' Large white flowers with numerous pink spots inside.

Hyacinthus orientalis 'Ostara' AGM
Family: Liliaceae Common name: Hyacinth

Originating from the Middle East, including Turkey, Syria and Lebanon, most people will have never seen the wild species since bulb breeders developed the hybrid, pot-plant varieties many years ago. However, they are fully hardy and can be grown successfully in most parts of the United Kingdom.

Flowers are carried in dense spikes up to 30cm (12in) tall, usually having 30–40 small tubular flowers 2.5cm (1in) long. Very fragrant, depending upon the variety, and lasting for several weeks particularly in cool weather. Leaves are dark green and strap-shaped, initially enclosing the flower spike. The leaves lengthen as the flower spike grows and eventually extend above the flower spike, up to a height of 40cm (16in).

Remove the flower spike as the flowers fade to ensure that food produced by the leaves is stored in the bulb for next year's display. Leave the foliage in place until it has completely died down.

In severe winters there may be some flower damage, especially if grown in pots or tubs and the compost becomes totally frozen. Slugs and snails can be a problem. Largest bulbs should be chosen for indoor or pot cultivation but smaller bulbs are suitable for planting in beds or borders in the autumn. Bulbs are generally sold by circumference, available up to 24cm (10in), but smaller bulbs can provide adequate displays.

Varieties & Forms

HYACINTHUS ORIENTALIS 'PINK PEARL' AGM Having pale-pink flowers with almost white edges to the petals.

HYACINTHUS ORIENTALIS 'BEN NEVIS' Double pure-white flowers on compact spikes.

HYACINTHUS ORIENTALIS 'CITY OF HAARLEM' AGM A late-flowering variety bearing large yellow flowers.

Daphne mezereum 'Bowles Variety'

Family: Thymelaeaceae Common name: Mezereon

The mezereon is endemic to Europe, including the United Kingdom, although it is rarely seen in the wild now. Found as far east as Turkey and Russia, it thrives in limestone areas and when grown in cottage-style gardens in chalky areas.

long and develop after the flowers have faded.

This vigorous shrub will eventually reach 1.6m (5ft). Plant in a moisture-retaining soil in full sun or light shade.

Varieties & Forms

DAPHNE MEZEREUM F. 'ALBA' Has beautiful, creamy-white, scented flowers.

DAPHNE MEZEREUM Var. RUBRUM A selection with dark red-purplish flowers.

DAPHNE MEZEREUM Var. 'AUTUMNALIS' Flowers in late autumn.

An upright-growing deciduous shrub, producing flowers before the leaves develop. Long-lasting flowers are pink or white, forming small clusters in February or March that hug the leafless stem, clothing up to 20cm (8in) of each stem. Star-shaped very fragrant flowers are approximately 8mm (½in) across, followed by bright-red glossy berries. These fruits are, unfortunately, very poisonous. Leaves are light-green, narrow, lance-shaped and up to 10cm (4in)

Stachyurus praecox AGM
Family: Stachyuraceae

Found in the wild on hillsides in Japan, this shrub flowers in February and March.

A tall spreading shrub with reddish stems growing up to 4m (13ft). During the winter pendulous racemes 10–15cm (4–6in) long are formed, arranged regularly along the branches and composed of numerous greenish flower buds. In favourable mild winter weather small flowers open, 8mm (½in) across. After flowering leaves emerge that are ovate, light-green and up to 15cm (6in) long.

Plant in a sheltered position, against a sunny wall is ideal. Provide a fertile soil rich in humus to prevent the roots drying out and encourage flower bud formation.

Varieties & Forms

STACHYURUS PRAECOX 'MAGPIE'
Compact, only growing to 2m (6ft) tall, this variety has irregular cream margins around the leaves.

37

SPRING

With springtime's uncertain temperatures and rainfall, include a variety of plant types for a guaranteed show of colour.

Weeks 10-21

The subtle change from winter flowering plants to those flowering in spring is not obvious. According to the Meteorological Office, in the temperate region in which we live, Spring is the months of March, April and May.

Obviously weather patterns still influence the flowering time and length of display. Generally long cold spells are rare in March and April, although the weather can be strangely very dry in March. These dry spells influence the onset of flowering and can shorten the display, but luckily more plants are in flower during spring than in any other season of the year.

The week in which the flowering commences also varies from year to year, so I have attempted to average out the potential flowering time. It is not foolproof and may not follow exactly the weeks stated. This period of the year is also the time when many of the plants detailed in the winter garden ultimately run out of steam. These include 'Winter Flowering Jasmine' *Jasminum nudiflorum* and *Viburnum x bodnantense*.

Some spring flowering shrubs, such as Plant 59, Choisya temata, *often have a good habit of having a second flowering flush later in the year, so it is useful to choose these and get more for your money.*

Narcissus 'February Gold' AGM

Family: Amaryllidaceae

Flowering in March, despite its common name, this early Narcissus has a neat growth habit but is fairly vigorous.

Golden-yellow flowers up to 7cm (3in) across are produced on 20cm (8in) stems. The stems continue to grow with the expanding foliage and can reach 30–35cm (12–14in) in height. The flowers are formed of a trumpet, about 5cm (2in) long, and six slightly reflexed perianth segments. Typical of many in this group, the flowers hang their heads due to a sharp angle between the stem and the head.

Clumps form rapidly, so lift and divide the bulbs every 4–5 years, as soon as the leaves have yellowed and withered during May or early June. Replant one and a half times as deep as the width of the bulb. If planting newly bought bulbs, plant in October or early November.

This variety is excellent for naturalizing in grass; do not mow until the foliage has completely died down. Narcissus flies, slugs and snails may cause problems.

Varieties & Forms

FEBRUARY SILVER Similar habit, but has slightly smaller creamy-white flowers with lemon-yellow trumpet.

JACK SNIPE Flowers in March, growing to a height of 25cm (10in) with creamy-white 'petals' and short yellow trumpets.

CHARITY MAY AGM Height up to 30cm (12in), flowers end of March. Reflexed lemon-yellow 'petals' and bright-yellow trumpet.

Corylopsis pauciflora AGM
Family: Hamamelidaceae

A deciduous shrub originating from Japan and Taiwan found growing on mountains, on the edge of forests, and flowering in March or April.

Flowering before the leaves appear in early spring, this shrub grows to a height of 2.5m (8ft). Numerous clusters of flowers, up to 3cm (2in) long, cover the shrub in a pale-yellow haze. Its flowering habit is typical of wind-pollinated plants, with numerous flowers producing vast quantities of pollen. The flowers are pale lemon-yellow and long lasting. After they have faded, light-green oval leaves form, growing up to 4cm (1½in) long.

Choose a partly shaded location and provide a fertile acid soil for the best results.

Varieties & Forms

CORYLOPSIS SINENSIS Similar but taller with longer racemes, up to 8cm (4in), of yellow flowers.

CORYLOPSIS Var. CALVESCENS F VEITCHIANA AGM Has yellow flowers with bright-red stamens.

Magnolia stellata AGM

Family: Magnoliaceae Common name: Star Magnolia

A low-growing magnolia that is suitable for even the smallest garden and can even be grown in a tub or container. Its origin is the woodlands and hillsides of Japan where it will grow to a height of 5m (16ft). As this plant flowers when still young, it is commonly planted in small gardens, but after many years it can outgrow its allocated space.

American botanist Dr G.R. Hall first discovered this plant in Japan. It was introduced to the UK via the USA, reaching here in 1877.

A very useful shrub, in suitable weather conditions it will start to flower in late February or early March. If frost is a problem, causing damage to the early flower buds, a second crop will be produced when conditions improve.

Slow growing, it will eventually reach 2.5m (8ft). The flowers have 12 or 16 pure-white petals with a typical cluster of dark-yellow stamens at the centre. Petals are up to 6cm (2½in) long and slowly droop to be reflexed (bent backwards); in some varieties they are tinged with pink. As the flowers fade, leaves unfurl from smaller silvery buds and grow to approximately 15cm (6in). They are pale green at first but darken with age.

Acid or neutral soil is required for good growth. Top dress annually to ensure an adequate supply of humus that will keep the roots moist and cool. Position the shrub in a sheltered position; some shade is welcomed and avoid a position where the early morning sun may damage the delicate flowers.

Varieties & Forms

MAGNOLIA STELLATA 'RUBRA' Has dark-pink flowers.

MAGNOLIA STELLATA 'WATER LILY' AGM With white flowers, approximately 13cm (5in) across, that consist of up to 32 petals.

Aubrieta x cultorum 'Hartswood Purple'

Family: Cruciferae Common name: Aubretia

The commonly grown garden varieties are not found in the wild, being hybrids produced by plant breeders over many years. Surprisingly these delightful floriferous carpeting plants belong to the cabbage family. They only grow 5cm (2in) high.

These plants have small hairy leaves up to 2cm (1in) long. Some are toothed while other varieties have entire (smooth-edged) leaves. The hairy nature of the leaves creates the impression that the plant is grey, which adds to the display of the small, simple, four-petalled flowers, that are 1cm (½in) across. In mild winters, flowering may commence as early as February, my earliest recording in recent years was 10th February.

Plant in rocky crevices or allow them to trail over dwarf walls where they are happiest in well-drained but fertile soil in full sun.

It can become invasive if allowed to grow unchecked, so trim after flowering with shears or secateurs.

Varieties & Forms

AUBRETIA x CULTORUM 'AUREOVARIEGATA' Has mauve flowers and gold-edged leaves.

AUBRETIA x CULTORUM 'JOY' Has double mauve flowers.

AUBRETIA x CULTORUM 'BRESSINGHAM PINK' Raised by British horticulturalist Alan Bloom 40 years ago. Has large clusters of double pink flowers.

Muscari botryoides

Family: Liliaceae Common name: Grape Hyacinth

This plant grows wild in Eastern Europe, Greece and Turkey. The common name describes the shape of the flower head – a little like a small bunch of grapes. An unusual habit of *M. botryoides* is that, after a short period of dormancy during the summer months, the foliage forms in the autumn and stays green during the winter ready to show off the flowers in spring.

The grass-like foliage grows to 20cm (8in) and flowering stems grow rapidly from the tuft of foliage, showing colour almost as soon as they appear. Eventually they grow to a height of 20–25cm (8–10in), producing flower clusters 5cm (2in) long in dense heads of tiny, blue tubular flowers approximately 1cm (½in) long; often the mouth is paler blue or white.

This plant multiplies rapidly and can become a nuisance if left undisturbed for many years. It is therefore best to lift clumps every 4–5 years, selecting the largest bulbs for replanting. The smaller bulbs can be discarded, given away to friends and neighbours, or planted in a new location to start a new colony. When purchasing new bulbs, plant as early as possible; September is preferable to enable them to commence growing.Shade is tolerated but they flower best in a sunny position in well-draining but moisture-retentive soil. Slugs and snails may damage flowers and flower stems.

Varieties & Forms

MUSCARI ARMENIACUM 'BLUE SPIKE' Leaves up to 30cm (12in); spikes 20cm (8in) long of dense, double, light-blue flowers.

MUSCARI LATIFOLIUM A single leaf encloses each flowering stem. Stems up to 25cm (10in) topped with a cluster of dark-violet flowers and a crown of paler sterile flowers.

MUSCARI MACROCARPUM Has fragrant, yellow, tubular flowers opening from purplish buds.

Prunus cerasifera 'Nigra' AGM

Family: Rosaceae Common name: Black Cherry Plum

P. cerasifera originated in southern parts of Eastern Europe, spreading across into Asia. It is known as 'Cherry Plum' as it produces small, sometimes edible, cherry-sized fruit. *P.c.* 'Nigra' is an ornamental leaved variety.

The flowers are bowl shaped with pink petals up to 2cm (1in) across. They are produced during April and although this plant is not usually grown for its flowers, they look attractive against the emerging dark-red foliage. Flowers last for a few weeks and slowly fade to white before the petals fall. Leaves are red when young and grow to 6cm (2½in), darkening to a deeper purple-red as they age. In some years the flowers are followed by small dark red edible fruits like small plums. In the autumn the foliage turns orange-red before falling. The tree grows quickly at first but slows as it ages, taking a number of years to reach its ultimate size of 8m (25ft).

This tree does best in full sun and likes a moisture-retentive soil. In common with many Prunus it is susceptible to a number of diseases including blossom wilt, scab and silver leaf. To lessen attacks of disease, do not prune during the winter dormant season.

Varieties & Forms

PRUNUS CERASIFERA (Common name Cherry Plum) Produces numerous white single flowers before the leaves, followed by edible red or yellow fruits.

Ribes sanguineum
Family: Grossulariaceae Common name: Flowering Currant

This woodland shrub is found in pine forests on the lower slopes of the Rocky Mountains along the west of the USA and Canada, as far north as British Columbia. Originally named by the Scottish botanist Archibald Menzies in 1793, it was introduced into the UK by another Scotsman, David Douglas, in 1826.

Very upright and growing to 2.6m (8ft), *R. sanguineum* can be hard pruned to keep the shrub tidy and within its allocated space.

All parts have an unpleasant smell when bruised. Flowers are produced in April, maybe earlier in mild weather, in hanging racemes of 15–20 small pink flowers. The dark-green leaves are long stalked and 4–5cm (1.5–2in) across with 3–5 lobes that have paler hairy undersides.

Depending upon weather conditions, flowers are followed by black berries with a white bloom. The berries are approximately 6mm (¼in) across. It will grow in a wide variety of soils and tolerates some shade, although flowering will be reduced in shady sites.

Pruning should be done after flowering. Remove older less vigorous branches down to ground level and shorten back newer flowered stems by about one-third.

Varieties & Forms

RIBES 'PULBOROUGH SCARLET' AGM An improved form of the species, having red flowers. Raised in Pulborough, Sussex in 1933, very vigorous growing to 3m (10ft).

'KING EDWARD VII' The darkest red of any variety with a slight spreading habit of up to 2m (6ft).

'TYDEMANS WHITE' AGM Has large clusters of creamy-white flowers.

Pulmonaria officinalis

Family: Boraginaceae Common name: Lungwort

Growing wild in many countries of mainland Europe, 'Lungwort' favours the edges of woodlands and hedgerows. The plant shown in the photograph is *P.* 'Lewis Palmer'.

This plant spreads via rhizomes that grow both under and above the ground. Its leaves are hairy and up to 15cm (6in) in length with silver markings; flower stems are also hairy and sparsely leaved. They bear racemes of tubular flowers and prominent clusters of green sepals.

Flowers are obvious almost as soon as the stems start to elongate. Individual flowers are approximately 2cm (¾in) long and in various shades of red, blue or white.

Preferring a moisture-retentive soil in light shade, this plant tolerates a wide range of conditions, although dry soils in full sun will shorten its life and flowering period.

Varieties & Forms

PULMONARIA OFFICINALIS 'SISSINGHURST WHITE' AGM Smaller, with white flowers.

PULMONARIA 'LEOPARD' Has very spotted leaves and red flowers.

PULMONARIA RUBRA AGM Almost unmarked green leaves. Pinkish-red flowers.

Chionodoxa forbesii

Family: Liliaceae Common name: Glory of the Snow

Found in the wild in Turkey, this plant grows on mountains and flowers at the end of winter and in early spring.

'Glory of the Snow' bulbs produce leaves and flowers at the same time. The buds open quickly to reveal star-shaped flowers, up to 2cm (¾in) across, that are pale blue with a white eye. The flower stems grow up to 20cm (8in) and carry up to 12 flowers. Leaves are dark green, linear and pointed. They grow taller than the flower stems when the flowers fade.

Plant these bulbs deeply in well-draining soil in a sunny position.

Dappled shade under deciduous trees is also acceptable. They naturalize well in grass as the foliage dies down quickly. Slugs and snails may be a problem in damp situations.

Varieties & Forms

C. FORBESII 'PINK GIANT' Has small pink flowers with a paler eye.

CHIONODOXA SARDENSIS AGM Flowers are pure blue with no white eye.

Magnolia x soulangeana
Family: Magnoliaceae

Of hybrid origin, this large shrub's parents are *M. denudata* and *M. lilliflora*. Many forms have been produced. Requiring plenty of room to develop, the shrub will grow to a height of 6m (20ft), often with a similar-sized spread if given the space. It can be grown as a tree with a single stem or allowed to produce multiple stems.

Large dark-green leaves up to 20cm (8in) long are produced after the early flowers. The flowers, variable both in size and colour, are mostly large and goblet-shaped with waxy petals up to 15cm (6in) long and pink, darkening in colour towards the base. They form in late winter, slowly opening to reveal a large cluster of yellow stamens, but rarely remain open except just as the petals fall; some remain unopened as the leaves emerge.

Plant this large shrub in an acid moisture-retaining soil in partial shade or a sunny position that is sheltered from cold drying winds. Following a hard frost, the early morning sun can damage the flowers, but unopened specimens usually escape. Only minimal pruning is required to remove dead branches or over-crowded stems.

Varieties & Forms

MAGNOLIA x SOULANGEANA 'ALBA SUPERBA' Upright with pure-white fragrant flowers that are slightly flushed with purple.

MAGNOLIA x SOULANGEANA 'LENNEI' AGM Has dark-purple flowers, 10cm (4in) across, with a white interior.

MAGNOLIA LILLIFLORA, A smaller shrub at up to 3m (10ft) tall. Produces deep-purple flowers in mid spring.

Anemone blanda AGM
Family: Ranunculaceae

A beautiful but fleeting plant that grows, flowers and seeds in a very short period of time. Originating from southern Europe across to Turkey, it flowers during March and April.

Stems emerge in early spring from knobbly brown underground tubers. These tubers are small, up to 2.5cm (1in) across, and irregular in shape. Once planted they are difficult to find so almost impossible to relocate.

Each stem grows to 15cm (6in) high and has one or two small palmate dark-green leaves. Each leaf is composed of three lobed leaflets approximately 3cm (1½in) across. Young leaves and stems are purplish topped with blue, pink, or white flowers consisting of 10–15 tepals (petals). Flowers are 4–5cm (1½in) across and open in bright sunshine. The centre has a golden-yellow cluster of stamens.

Plant in moisture-retentive soil in partial shade under trees.

Varieties & Forms

ANEMONE BLANDA 'ATROCAERULEA' Dark-blue flowers.

ANEMONE BLANDA 'WHITE SPLENDOUR' AGM Large white flowers with a pink tinge.

ANEMONE BLANDA 'CHARMER' With dark-pink flowers.

Chaenomeles speciosa 'Etna'
Family: Rosaceae Common name: Flowering Quince

C. speciosa is originally from China and is fully hardy in the United Kingdom. Grown for its decorative early flowers, it then produces leaves and subsequent ornamental, aromatic, greenish-yellow fruits, known as quince. The variety shown is a hybrid of garden origin.

The cup-shaped flowers have five petals and vary in colour; the variety shown has red buds opening to crimson flowers in clusters of up to six, with bright yellow stamens.

Leaves form once flowering is over. They are a bright glossy green, 5–8cm (2-3in) long, and drop early in the autumn when the very aromatic fruits can be seen. These fruits, up to 8cm (3in) long, remain amongst the thorny branches for many months – often still apparent as the new flowers are in bud in January and February. The fruits are very hard but can be cooked to make quince jelly or used as a source of pectin in order to set other preserves.

The shrub can be trained against a wall or fence and attains a height of 2.5m (8ft). It prefers a neutral to an acid soil but will tolerate some chalk. Position in full sun or light shade to encourage flowering in a fertile well-draining soil.

Only prune to shape immediately after flowering. Remove some older wood annually otherwise the lower branches may become bare and devoid of any flowers.

Varieties & Forms

CHAENOMELES SPECIOSA 'MOERLOOSEI' AGM This has pink flower buds that open to whitish flowers.

CHAENOMELES 'PHYLLIS MOORE' Has clusters of dark-pink flowers.

Ipheion uniflorum
Family: Alliaceae

From the hills and rocky mountains of South America including Argentina and Uruguay.

A bulbous plant related to allium, *I. uniflorum* has only a short period of dormancy. It produces grass-like foliage, smelling slightly of onions, in the autumn. The leaves are bluish-green, strap shaped and up to 25cm (10in) long.

The plant persists throughout the winter, producing solitary star-shaped flowers in late winter. The main flowering period is March to April; the 3cm (1¼in) flowers are pale silvery-blue. Petals often have a darker midrib, but this is variable. Clumps increase rapidly and regular division is recommended to remove older bulbs, which flower less.

Well-drained soil in a sunny position is favoured, preferably at the base of a hedge or among the roots of deciduous trees.

Some bulbs and flowers may be damaged in very frosty conditions, so mulch with a layer of compost or leaf mould. Slugs and snails may damage the flowers.

Varieties & Forms

IPHEION UNIFLORUM 'ALBUM' Has pure-white flowers.

IPHEION UNIFLORUM 'WISLEY BLUE' AGM Has the best coloured flowers — a beautiful lilac-blue.

Skimmia japonica

Family: Rutaceae

An evergreen shrub introduced from China, Japan and other countries of southeast Asia into the UK by the Scottish botanist Robert Fortune. The photograph above shows S.*japonica* 'Fructu Albo'.

The dark-green oval leaves of this shrub are thick, leathery and up to 10cm (4in) long. In April and May it produces dense panicles of fragrant greenish-white flowers, sometimes tinged with pink.

Male and female plants are needed to produce berries, which follow the flowers on the female plants. These shiny, red, spherical fruits are 8mm (½in) across and grow in clusters.

If left unpruned, *S. japonica* can grow to 6m (20ft), but this is extremely unusual. There are many selected forms and usually the selections are easier to obtain from garden centres and nurseries.

Varieties & Forms

SKIMMIA JAPONICA 'RUBELLA' AGM A male clone, exhibiting a reddish colour in new leaves, shoots and flower stems. Scented flowers open to pale pink. Found wild in China; introduced to UK in the 19th century.

SKIMMIA JAPONICA SUBSP. REEVESIANA Hermaphrodite with narrower leaves. Dark-red oval fruits.

SKIMMIA x CONFUSA 'KEW GREEN' AGM Compact growth, greenish-white very fragrant male flowers in spring.

Anemone nemerosa AGM

Family: Ranunculaceae Common name: Wood anemone

Found naturally in the woodlands of Europe including the United Kingdom and Ireland.

This creeping plant spreads from thin brown underground rhizomes. It produces flowering and non-flowering stems in early April. These are reddish and produce dark-green palmate leaves that are up to 4cm (1½in) across.

Pinkish flower buds, one per stem, open to almost white flowers up to 3cm (1in) with up to eight tepals (petals) and a central tuft of creamy-white stamens. Flowers are followed by seeds that develop quickly, helping to provide rapid colonization in suitable areas.

Moisture-retentive soil in a shady position is preferrable, under deciduous trees is ideal. Top dress annually with leaf mould or well-rotted garden compost. Slugs and snails may damage the flowers.

Varieties & Forms

ANEMONE NEMEROSA 'VESTAL' AGM Has double flowers 2.5cm (1in) across.

ANEMONE NEMEROSA 'BLUE BONNET' Has deep-blue flowers 3–4cm (1–1½in) across. Flowers later.

Ranunculus ficaria

Family: Ranunculaceae Common name: Lesser Celandine

A British native wild flower and a very attractive early flowering plant when used in the correct location. The plant develops from small underground tubers.

Golden-yellow flowers up to 2.5cm (1in) across are usually produced in March and April, although occasionally in mild wintry weather in a sheltered situation I have recorded the plant flowering in January. The leaves are dark green, up to 5cm (2in) across, with darker markings and petioles approximately 8cm (3in) long.

The plant flourishes in damp and shady conditions. It can sometimes become a nuisance, due to the problem of small tubers becoming detached and forming a new plant. To avoid this, restrict the amount of space allocated to it and do not cultivate the area, which would spread the tubers.

Varieties & Forms

RANUNCULUS FICARIA 'SALMON'S WHITE' Has white flowers.

RANUNCULUS FICARIA 'BRAZEN HUSSY' Dark-bronzed foliage with golden flowers.

RANUNCULUS FICARIA 'COLLARETTE' Has double flowers.

Mahonia aquifolium

Family: Berberidaceae Common name: Oregon Grape

Grows wild in the western states of the USA and Canada, including Oregon, from which it takes its common name. Discovered by one of the world's great plant collectors, David Douglas, in 1825.

This evergreen shrub grows to approximately 1.5m (5ft), spreading by suckers. Its leaves are pinnate, having 3–5 pairs of leaflets. They are glossy-green tinged with red, particularly when young, and have sharply pointed toothed edges, almost like holly leaves. Overall leaves are up to 25cm (10in) long and 10cm (4in) wide, usually turning reddish in the winter months.

The suckering growth habit may sometimes, in ideal growing conditions, become a nuisance. An abundance of dense 9cm (4in) long racemes of golden-yellow flowers are produced in early spring from buds that are very obvious during the winter. These are followed by bunches of fruit (like small grapes), black with a grey bloom.

M. aquifolium will grow in any fertile soil in sun for maximum flowering, but is also suitable for ground cover in shady situations.

Varieties & Forms

MAHONIA REPENS 'ROTUNDIFOLIA' Similar habit, growing up to 1.5m (4–5ft) with rounded leaflets.

MAHONIA AQUIFOLIUM 'APOLLO' A more compact habit, up to 60cm (2ft)

MAHONIA AQUIFOLIUM 'ORANGE FLAME' Good colour leaves in autumn, turning red in winter.

Amelanchier lamarckii AGM

Family: Rosaceae Common name: Snowy Mespilus

A shrub that is not known in the wild but has been naturalized throughout Europe. Can be grown as a tree when trained on a single stem.

This large shrub or small tree can grow to 10m (30ft). It has oblong leaves that are bronze when new, turning dark green as the season advances. It will often produce a splendid display of autumn colour. Leaves are up to 6cm (2½in) long and 3cm (1in) wide.

In April and May, racemes of small pinkish-white flowers form. They are sometimes followed by sweet and juicy edible fruits, 7–10mm (½in) in diameter.

Plant in full sun or a lightly shaded situation in an acid, well-draining but moisture-retentive soil. Pruning is only needed to shape the shrub and to remove dead or over-crowded shoots. Being a member of the rose family, this plant can be infected by fireblight disease.

Varieties & Forms

AMELANCHIER 'BALLERINA' AGM Growing up to 6m (19ft) it has glossy leaves and edible blue-black fruits.

AMELANCHIER x GRANDIFLORA 'AUTUMN BRILLIANCE' A vigorous large shrub or small tree up to 8m (25ft) tall.

Pieris japonica
Family: Ericaceae Common name: Lily of the Valley bush

An evergreen shrub, originating from Japan and Himalayan regions of China. The variety shown is *P. j.* 'Grayswood', which was raised at a garden in Surrey called Grayswood.

Growing up to 4m (13ft) tall, this shrub has a compact habit when young with elliptic, bright-green, glossy leaves (often pinkish-red when young) that grow to 10cm (4in) long. Young shoots may be damaged by late frosts.

Large panicles of flowers develop in the winter and open in early spring to reveal creamy-white, urn-shaped flowers approximately 1cm (½in) long. They are slightly scented and long-lasting, often still open as the new pink foliage is produced.

The shrub requires acid soil that is well-draining but with an adequate supply of organic material.

The photograph aqbove was taken on 12th March 2011 in Windsor Great Park.

Varieties & Forms

PIERIS JAPONICA 'FLAMINGO'
A modern selection with short panicles of deep-pink flowers.

PIERIS 'FOREST FLAME' AGM
Probably the most well-known variety, the young shoots create a spectacular display of pink and red.

PIERIS JAPONICA 'VARIEGATA'
Slow growing and useful in a small garden. Leaves have cream margins but flowers are sparse.

Caltha palustris AGM

Family: Ranunculaceae Common name: Marsh Marigold

Widely distributed throughout the Northern hemisphere, including the United Kingdom. An aquatic plant growing in wet soils on the margins of ponds or slow-moving streams.

The spreading hollow stems have kidney-shaped, dark-green, glossy leaves, up to 15cm (6in) across. Flowering stems grow up to 50cm (18in) long and produce flowers over a period of many weeks.

The yellow flowers are up to 5cm (2in) across, have five petals and are more or less star shaped. Although best grown as a marginal aquatic, it will often grow happily in a mixed border with a moisture-retentive soil and a good supply of organic material.

Varieties & Forms

CALTHA PALUSTRIS Var. ALBA Has whitish flowers with a greenish-yellow centre of stamens.

CALTHA PALUSTRIS 'FLORE PLENO' AGM Has fully double yellow flowers and a more compact habit.

Primula denticulata AGM

Family: Primulaceae Common name: Drumstick Primula

A herbaceous perennial that grows wild in central parts of Asia and on the mountains of Afghanistan and China.

The leaves of this plant form in rosettes that are tightly curled during the winter. When they unfurl, they are light-green and oblong with a toothed edge. They grow to 25cm (10in) long and 5–7cm (2–3in) wide. A white farina (wax-like deposit) is found on the underside of the leaves and at the central growing point of each of the rosettes.

Flower stems emerge in late winter and early spring, extending during flowering to a height of approximately 40cm (16in). Pale-purple flowers with a yellow eye form in dense spherical clusters and grow to 6cm (2½in) across.

Grow in fertile moist soil that will not dry out during the summer months and top dress annually with garden compost. Divide these plants every few years to retain vigorous growth.

New plants can be raised from seed; the seedlings will produce flowers of different colours.

Varieties & Forms

PRIMULA Var. ALBA Flowers are white with a yellow eye.

PRIMULA DENTICULATA 'RUBRA' With reddish-purple stems and flowers.

Erica arborea 'Alpina' AGM

Family: Ericaceae Common name: Tree Heath

A wide range of natural habitats include the Canary Islands, Spain and southern France across to the Black Sea; it also grows in North Africa. Wood from the 'Tree Heath' has been used for many purposes including the bowl of smoking pipes.

This shrub produces flowers in Mediterranean areas from March through until early May. In the UK, flowering depends upon the weather, being delayed by cold frosty conditions.

Although the shrub will eventually form a small tree, reaching a height of 7m (23ft), in this country it is more usual to see specimens around a maximum of 4m (13ft) tall. It is very upright and densely branched with small, dark-green, needle-like leaves approximately 1.5cm (½in) long.

The white flowers form in long spikes from axillary buds (at the junction of the stem and the leaf stalk), up to 5mm (¼in) long. The variety 'Alpina' is hardier than other E. arborea forms, and will grow successfully in most parts of the UK. Branches are brittle and may be damaged by the weight of snow. Prune only to shape and keep the plant upright, do not prune into older wood as new growth will not develop on old woody branches.

Varieties & Forms

ERICA ARBOREA 'ALBERT'S GOLD' AGM Compact up to 2m (6ft) with golden foliage but few flowers.

ERICA x VEITCHII Hybrid of *E. arborea* and *E. lusitanica* that is tolerant of slightly alkaline soils. Flowers February to May. Up to 2.5m (8ft).

Ulex europaeus

Family: Leguminosae Common name: Common Gorse

A common shrub growing throughout Europe, including the United Kingdom and Ireland, and into North Africa. Un-pruned the shrub grows tall and straggly. The wood is brittle and top-heavy branches break under the weight of new growth.

axils. They are heavily scented, smelling of almonds or coconut.

Large numbers of seed pods up to 5cm (2in) long follow the flowers, quickly turning brownish-grey. During warm sunny periods, the pods twist and split violently with a loud click, propelling the seeds in all directions.

A sunny position in acid or neutral soil gives the best flowering display. Pruning is recommended immediately after flowering in May due to the untidy growth habit; shears are often the best method.

Flowering can be spasmodic commencing in the autumn, continuing intermittently during the winter and with a final burst of colour from March to May. The bright, pea-shaped flowers provide a showy display of golden-yellow in the main flowering period, followed by numerous seed pods.

This 2.5m (8ft) shrub provides a good deterrent to animals and human trespassers, so it is useful around the margins or perimeters of the garden. Regular pruning can keep it within bounds.

Leaves have been modified to green spines, about 2.5cm (1in) long, produced on green stems also tipped with spines. Flowers are a bright golden-yellow approximately 2cm (¾in) produced in the leaf

Varieties & Forms

ULEX EUROPAEUS 'FLORE PLENO' AGM Has double flowers; no seeds are produced.

ULEX EUROPAEUS 'STRICTUS' Fewer spines, and a more upright habit.

ULEX GALLII Similar, but only grows to 1.2m (4ft), flowering July–September.

GENISTA HISPANICA More compact, only attaining 50cm (20in). Flowers April–May.

Iberis sempervirens

Family: Cruciferae Common name: Perennial Candytuft

Grows wild in southern Europe, including Spain, France, Greece and Italy, this sub-shrub is usually found growing in a calcareous soil.

This evergreen sub-shrub may lose most of its leaves in severe winters. In mild weather, however, it will continue to flower spasmodically, even in December.

The dark-green leaves are narrow, linear (strap-shaped) and up to 4cm (1½in) long. In April and May slightly scented white flowers, arranged in flattened racemes, up to 4cm (1½in) across. Each flower has four petals, two of which are usually larger than the others. The plant grows to a height of 30cm (12in) with a spread of up to 60cm (2ft).

It will grow in a wide range of soil types in all regions of the UK. It can be grown in a rock garden or in a dry-stone wall where it will cascade over the stones to provide a carpet of white flowers. Clipping annually will prevent *I. sempervirens* from becoming untidy or out-growing its allotted space.

Varieties & Forms

IBERIS SAXATILIS Flowers in late spring, low growing with many heads of small white flowers.

IBERIS AMARA 'ICEBERG' Up to 40cm (16in) high, long racemes (see glossary) of numerous pure-white flowers.

IBERIS AMARA 'PINNACLE' Very fragrant white flowers.

Spiraea arguta

Family: Rosaceae Common name: Bridal Wreath

A very popular shrub, of unknown origin, it has been in cultivation for a long time. In Japan the common name is 'Snow Willow' because of its arching stems covered in white blossom.

Growing to a height of 2.5m (8ft) if allowed to go un-pruned, this deciduous shrub produces leaves early in the year at the same time as its flowers.

In April and early May, masses of small white flowers are formed in clusters on short leafy shoots, appearing on un-flowered branches from the previous year. Leaves are up to 4cm (1½in) long and bright-green with a toothed margin.

To retain vigorous growth, prune to remove branches that are more than three or four years old.

Prefers a fertile well-draining soil in a sunny position. Although fully hardy, late spring frosts may damage young leaves, but the plant will soon recover.

Varieties & Forms

SPIRAEA NIPPONICA 'SNOWMOUND' AGM A spreading deciduous shrub with masses of small white flowers in June.

SPIRAEA JAPONICA 'LITTLE PRINCESS' Forms a dense mound of pink flowers, growing to a height of 50cm (20in).

Berberis darwinii AGM

Family: Berberidaceae Common name: Holly Leaved Barberry

Growing wild in South America, including Argentina and Chile, this is one of the most popular Barberries. This shrub was discovered by Darwin during the voyage of HMS *Beagle* in 1835, but was not cultivated in the UK until 1894.

This upright shrub can reach 3m (10ft), but is usually less in gardens. The strong vigorous stems are covered with small, evergreen, glossy leaves with spiny margins, like tiny holly leaves, 2–4cm (1–1½in) long. At the base of each leaf are typically three short spines. In April and May, pendulous racemes of golden-orange flowers each up to 6mm (¼in) long form in clusters of up to 30. These are followed by round blue-black berries covered in a glaucous (bluish-green) bloom.

It prefers a well-drained soil in full sun, producing fewer flowers in shady positions. Prune after flowering to shorten vigorous growth, removing older flowered branches to maintain a balance of older and new growth.

Varieties & Forms

BERBERIS Var. FLAME Larger leaves, orange-red flowers and a more compact habit. Up to 1.5m (5ft).

BERBERIS x LOLOGENSIS 'APRICOT QUEEN' AGM A hybrid from *B. darwinii* and *B. linearifolia*. Large glossy leaves and clusters of orange yellow flowers in late spring.

Erythronium americanum
Family: Liliaceae Common name: Yellow Adder's Tongue

Many species of *Erythronium* originate from North America; this species is also commonly known as the 'American Trout Lily', because of the fish-like leaf shape and markings.

Growing from strange-shaped knobbly bulbs this plant produces in early spring, leaves that are strap-shaped, up to 15cm (6in) long, marked with purple-brown blotches. Flower stems 20–25cm (8–10in) high carry solitary yellow flowers approximately 5cm (2in) across, nodding with reflexed pointed tepals and bright-yellow or brown downward-pointing stamens. After flowering, the leaves rapidly disappear, especially when there is a very dry spring.

Grow in light to heavy shade, under deciduous trees is often the best situation. Top dress annually with leaf mould or well-rotted garden compost to ensure that the bulbs do not dry out during the long dormant period.

Slugs and snails may be a problem for this plant. Buy bulbs from a reputable supplier or buy actively growing plants in pots and then plant deeply.

Varieties & Forms

ERYTHRONIUM DENS-CANIS A European native, with a single pink or violet flower on each stem, only growing to 15cm (6in) high.

ERYTHRONIUM CALIFORNICUM 'WHITE BEAUTY' Has creamy white flowers and a vigorous habit. Up to 30cm (12in) high.

Euphorbia polychroma AGM
Family: Euphorbiaceae

A native of many European countries including Germany, Romania and Bulgaria where it is usually found growing in alkaline soils on woodland edges.

Many stems are produced from a woody rootstock in early spring, growing up to 35cm (14in) high.

Oblong leaves are up to 5cm (2in) long, light green and hairy. The flower heads, up to 6cm (2½in) across are typical euphorbia form, consisting of yellow cyathia (false flowers) surrounded by yellowish-green bracts (the part of the plant just below the petals). Euphorbia floral parts are not clearly recognisable flowers, lacking petals or sepals. They give a bright golden appearance for several weeks.

Plant in fertile soil in a sunny or partly shaded position.

Varieties & Forms

EUPHORBIA POLYCHROMA 'CANDY' Has purplish stems and leaves with paler-yellow cyathia (false flowers).

EUPHORBIA PALUSTRIS AGM Grows up to 90cm (3ft) high with clusters of yellow cyathia (false flowers) 15cm (6in) across. Good autumn colour.

Cytisus x praecox

Family: Leguminosae

A short-lived shrub of garden origin, its parents being *C. multiflorus* and *C. purgans*.

The shrub is deciduous and grows to a height of 1.2m (4ft) with graceful arching stems. Clusters of pale-yellow, typically legume-like flowers are formed in leaf axils. The flowers are fragrant and 1–2cm (½–¾in) long. Small simple leaves are produced after flowering.

C. x praecox prefers a well-draining soil in full sun, growing best in acid soils. Prune with shears or secateurs immediately after flowering, but be careful not to prune into older wood.

Varieties & Forms

CYSTISUS 'ALLGOLD' AGM Has dark-yellow flowers.

CYSTISUS 'WARMINSTER' AGM Known as the 'Warminster Broom' having pale-cream to yellow flowers.

Clematis montana 'Rubens'

Family: Ranunculaceae

A very vigorous clematis suitable for rapid covering of objects which require screening or hiding. Can successfully climb through trees and large shrubs, but in the wrong situation it will dominate as it can easily grow to 8m (25ft) in one season.

Flowers are produced in great numbers on one-year-old wood or older, although the older the stem, the fewer the flowers produced. They consist of four petals, up to 8cm (3in) across, opening from dark-pink buds. Individually they are short lived, lasting three or four days, but the central tuft persists for several weeks, to be followed by the seed.

The seeds (usually sterile) are produced at the end of feathery silver structures, giving the plant extra interest. Leaves are in opposite pairs, the long leaf stalk is used as a tendril, twisting to cling to supports to hold the weight of the ever-lengthening stems. The young stems are reddish.

This climber is not very fussy as to the type of soil and is resistent to clematis wilt, the scourge of growing clematis. The only pest that is likely to be encountered is aphid. Select a named cultivar rather than *C montana*, as the wild species is very variable, rampant and produces few flowers.

Aphids may be troublesome in certain seasons, damaging flowers and growing tips. Prune to remove older flowered stems but do not prune too hard or you will encourage excess growth at the expense of flowers.

Varieties & Forms

CLEMATIS MONTANA 'PINK PERFECTION' Purplish green young leaves with fragrant pink flowers.

CLEMATIS MONTANA f. GRANDIFLORA AGM Large white flowers, a very vigorous form.

Narcissus 'Precocious'
Family Amaryllidaceae

Classified in Division 1 of the narcissus classification system, this is a beautiful large-flowered, pure-white form, flowering late in the season.

Has dark-green foliage that grows up to 35cm (15in) tall. The flowers are up to 7.5cm (3½in) across and are produced in late April and early May. Flowers are white with a small lemon-yellow trumpet. This variety is suitable for naturalising in grass or for mass planting under deciduous trees.

Remove leaves as soon as they have yellowed and are lying on the ground, as this reduces attacks of narcissus fly. This pest lays its eggs in the ground close to the bulb and is attracted by the smell of dying leaves.

Lift clumps of bulbs every four or five years, divide and replant in

Varieties & Forms

NARCISSUS 'PANACHE' One of the largest of the white-flowered varieties. Flowers, appearing in April, are up to 11cm (4½in) across.

NARCISSUS 'SATIN PINK' (Division 2) Flowers are up to 12cm (5in) across, with white perianth segments and pale-pink cups.

ones or twos, position the bulbs approximately 8cm (3½in) deep. This is best done after flowering when any foliage has died down; discard rotten or diseased bulbs.

Choisya ternata AGM
Family: Rutaceae Common name: Mexican Orange Blossom

As the common name suggests, this evergreen shrub originates from Mexico. The plant has pungent leaves and very fragrant flowers produced in two flushes.

The main flowering period is April, but often a second flowering occurs in September or October. Leaves are dark green and glossy with an unusual pungent aroma. Wide leaf petioles consisting of three to five leaflets, overall 7.5cm (3in) across. Flowers are produced in terminal clusters of up to 20 individual flowers. Individual flowers are white and star shaped with five petals and strongly fragrant. Flowering during early April to May, there is, in some years, a second flowering in September, although there are usually not as many flowers produced as in the spring.

Bright sunshine will sometimes spoil the dark-green leaves so position in a situation with light shade. Mulch annually to keep the fleshy roots well covered. Frost may sometimes damage the growing points and flower buds. Prune only to keep the shrub in shape and contain occasional vigorous shoots.

Occasionally, die back of stems may occur; prune them out immediately to prevent the onset of 'coral spot' disease.

Varieties & Forms

CHOISYA 'AZTEC PEARL' AGM Has a neat habit with very narrow leaflets; flowers well.

CHOISYA TERNATA 'SUNDANCE' AGM This variety has yellow-green foliage, to brighten up a shady corner, but produces few flowers.

Paeonia mlokosewitschii AGM

Family: Ranunculaceae Common name: Caucasian Peony

Originating from the Caucasus mountains where it grows amongst deciduous trees in woodlands, flowering as the trees burst into leaf.

Flowers are a beautiful bowl-shape, pale yellow and 8–12cm (3–5in) across, with a large cluster of golden yellow stamens at their centre. Unfortunately in keeping with many forms of paeony the flowers are short lived. Stems grow to a height of 60cm (24in) and carry light-green glossy leaves, sometimes grey-green beneath. Leaves are composed of up to six leaflets and are up to 20cm (8in) long. In autumn the leaves often turn shades of red and the seed pods can also be attractive, turning dark red and splitting to reveal black shiny seeds.

Grow in fertile soil, rich in organic material to retain moisture, in a sunny position. Plants may take some time to settle into new positions as they resent disturbance; do not plant too deeply.

Rhododendron yakushimanum
Family: Ericaceae

An evergreen shrub from Japan, discovered on the island of Yakushima, on mountainsides in the rain forest.

Will grow to 2.5m (8ft) but usually less, as cultivated forms have been selected to be compact. The leaves are dark green with rolled edges, approximately 14cm (5in) long. Their undersides are covered in a thick light-brown indumentum (fine hairs or scales). Young leaves have a light covering of indumentum on the upper surface, but this disappears after a few weeks.

Flowers are produced in April or May, in terminal clusters of up to 12 flowers. Opening from dark-pink buds, they are tubular, 2–4cm (1–2in) long and fade to pale pink or white as they age.

One of the easiest rhododendrons to grow, this shrub generally flowers year after year. As with most rhododendrons, an acid soil is required for successful growth and a light shady position is best. This variety has often been used in breeding programmes because of its attractive qualities.

Recent hybrids

'KOICHIRO WADA' Has white flowers opening from pink buds.

'OVERSTREET' Is similar but with narrow leaves.

Genista lydia AGM

Family: Leguminosae

From Eastern European countries including Greece and
Turkey, this free-flowering shrub useful as ground cover.

Forms a compact shrub that grows
up to 90cm (3ft) tall. The golden-
yellow flowers are produced over
several weeks during April and
May, found in short racemes 2–4cm
(1–2in) long on side branches.
Stems are arching, congested and
appear to be thorny but there
are no spines, only short stiff
branches. Leaves are small – almost
insignificant at 8–10mm (½in) long.
  Plant in well-draining soil in a
sunny position, where the shrub

Varieties & Forms

GENISTA HISPANICA More compact,
with short spines and terminal racemes
of golden-yellow flowers.

can often be used to best
advantage cascading over a wall
or to cover a steeply sloping section
of garden.

Limnanthes douglasii AGM

Family: Limnanthaceae Common name: Poached Egg Plant

This annual earns its place in the book as it requires only little effort to produce an effective display year after year. Originating from California, it establishes quite easily in most parts of the United Kingdom and is fully hardy. Seeds germinate readily if allowed to remain on the plant until ripe.

This carpeting plant grows to only 15cm (6in) high but may spread up to 40cm (16in). It is very free flowering except in wet weather. The light-green, feathery, divided leaves are 15cm (6in) long forming a central rosette until flowering time. The flowers are cup-shaped, 2.5cm (1in) across, and have five white petals with bright-yellow centres, looking like poached eggs. They are numerous but short lived.

Allow seeds to mature on the plant, then remove the plants ensuring that some seeds fall to the ground. Lightly fork over the soil surface to cover the seeds, which will germinate as soon as there is sufficient moisture. The plants will over-winter as an attractive ground cover until the following spring when a new crop of flowers will be formed. Newly purchased seeds can take several weeks to germinate if sown in spring, dependent upon weather conditions.

Grow in a sunny position and ensure that the soil has plenty of organic matter as a dry soil will curtail flowering. Alternatively incorporate water-retaining crystals into the top 10cm (4in) of soil.

Varieties & Forms

LIMNANTHES DOUGLASII VAR. SULPHUREA
An all-yellow flowered form that is occasionally produced and can be bought for novelty.

SUMMER

Flowering plants abound, but consider their colour and form for surprising or unusual displays.

Weeks 22-37

The summer months of June, July and August, are generally when people spend as much time as possible in the garden – long days and warm evenings are hoped for. However this is not necessarily the time of year when the best weather can be expected. July can often be a month of high rainfall and I have recorded almost 150mm (6in) of precipitation in the month of July on several occasions over the last 10 years. Many places in the UK were flooded in July 2007.

Luckily the summer months are a time of plenty with regard to shrubs, herbaceous perennials and seasonal bedding plants. Gardeners therefore have lots of choice and it has been relatively easy for me to select approximately 40 plants for this period of the year. I have attempted to provide a balance of popular plants, readily available in garden centres, and assessed by recording the number of gardens in which they can be found growing. At the same time I have tried to choose plants with good all-round attributes, not just flowers.

The summer months are generally the time of year when flowering shrubs are fewer and herbaceous perennials commence their flowering season. Those shrubs that do flower often have a short flowering period, whereas the herbaceous perennials in the garden often produce flowers over an extended length of time.

Astrantia maxima, *Hatties Pincushion (plant 83), the flower heads can be dried for flower arranging.*

Malus 'Evereste' AGM

Family: Rosaceae Common name: Crab Apple

A medium-sized conical-shaped deciduous tree, suitable only for the larger garden, to allow it to develop its true potential.

Spreading branches may extend up to 5m (16ft) and eventually this tree may grow to 8m (25ft) high. Oval leaves are dark green approximately 9–11cm (3–4in) long and they turn yellow in autumn before leaf fall. Dark-pink buds form in spring, opening to pure-white flowers, cup-shaped and up to 3cm (1¼in) across in clusters of five to eight.

Following flowering, the fruits 'crab apples' form, approximately 3cm (1¼in) across and yellow and red in colour. Ideal as a specimen tree in a lawn or in a border in full sun. Minimal pruning is needed in order to establish a well-spaced branch shape with an open centre. Pruning is best in late summer, when wounds heal quicker so are less likely to bleed.

Varieties & Forms

MALUS 'LEMOINEI' Reddish-purple leaves and dark-red flowers in April and May, sometimes followed by purplish-red fruits.

MALUS 'KATHERINE' AGM Double pale-pink flowers that change to white in April and May.

Iris sibirica

Family: Iridaceae Common name: Siberian Iris

Originally from Eastern Europe, Turkey and Russia, where it flourishes in wet meadows. It has been used as a parent of many modern hybrids.

Producing narrow spear-shaped leaves up to 60cm (24in) tall and only 1cm (½in) wide from a rhizomatous rootstock. In May and June, the stems carry three to five flowers that extend above the foliage. The flowers are without beards, purplish blue with darker purple markings on the fall petals and approximately 5cm (2in) across.

Grow in moist soil by ponds or stream edges or in a sunny area. Alternatively, grow in a border where the soil has a good supply of organic material to prevent the soil drying out in spring or summer.

Varieties & Forms

IRIS SIBIRICA F ALBA Has white flowers with yellow markings on the fall petals.

IRIS SIBIRICA 'SKYWINGS' A modern hybrid, has pale-violet flowers with yellow and purple markings on the fall petals.

Geranium sanguineum

Family: Geraniaceae Common name: Bloody Cranesbill

Native of Europe including Ireland and Scotland. The numerous species of hardy geraniums all have the common name cranesbill due to the shape of the plant's seed mechanism.

Many geraniums have long flowering periods often throughout April to August and sometimes well into the autumn if older flowered stems are removed. *G. sanguineum* is no exception.

The small leaves are dark green and deeply divided with five to seven lobes and approximately 4cm (1½in) across. The flowers are deep pink or red with five petals and approximately 3cm (1¼in) across. Plants are low-growing with short stems up to 30cm (12in) high rising from an underground rootstock. Creeping underground and appearing in new locations is a habit of this species and seedlings often occur so it is essential to keep this plant under control. In the wild the plant thrives in sunny situations among rocky outcrops in a wide variety of soils including alkaline, but is equally at home in sandy soils where it flowers profusely.

Trim with shears immediately after the main flowering period has passed; new shoots will grow to produce another crop of flowers.

Varieties & Forms

GERANIUM SANGUINEUM 'ALBUM' AGM Not as vigorous with white flowers.

Phlomis fruticosa

Family: Labiatae Common name: Jerusalem Sage

Found in the wild in the Mediterranean region, including Southern Europe and North Africa.

An evergreen shrub growing to 1.2m (4ft). Typically labiate with square stems and sage-like aromatic leaves, up to 8cm (3½in) long and wrinkled green with grey undersides. In May and June, whorls of yellow flowers clustered around the stems are produced. The flowers are tubular shaped with a distinct hood approximately 2.5cm (1in) long.

Grow in a fertile soil, but it will withstand some drought. Prune after flowering to shorten flowered stems and encourage the formation of new stems which will flower the following year.

Varieties & Forms

PHLOMIS RUSSELLIANA AGM
Herbaceous perennial plant growing from a woody rootstock. Many flowering stems up to 90cm (36in) are formed over a period of several weeks. Pale lemon-yellow flowers in large whorls around the stems.

Escallonia 'Apple Blossom' AGM

Family: Escalloniaceae

An evergreen shrub with small leaves and a profusion of pink flowers that can be successfully used as a screen or hedge.

Having a maximum height of 2.5m (8ft), this is an upright growing shrub. Small elliptic dark-green glossy leaves 3–4cm (1–1½in) long give it an attractive appearance all year round. In late spring and early summer, numerous racemes of pink flowers, up to 7cm (3in) long, are produced. Flowers open from dark-pink buds to reveal paler interiors, reminiscent of 'apple blossom'.

This shrub will grow well in most types of soil in a sunny position. Prune after flowering to remove old flowered stems and to keep the growth open by removing congested branches.

Varieties & Forms

ESCALLONIA 'PRIDE OF DONARD' AGM Similar in growth but has larger very dark-pink flowers.

ESCALLONIA IVEYI AGM Flowers later and has white flowers (see Plant 123).

Prunus lusitanica AGM

Family: Rosaceae Common name: Portuguese Laurel

A native of Spain, Portugal, the south of France and Madeira, growing up to 20m (66ft) in the wild, *P. lusitanica* is often grown as a screen. It does not usually reach this height in the UK, where it is sometimes slow to establish but then makes up for lost time.

This evergreen shrub's oval-shaped leaves are a glossy dark-green colour, up to 13cm (5¼in) long, with slightly waved edges and red petioles. During May and June, numerous narrow racemes up to 20cm (8in) long of fragrant white flowers are produced, followed by red cherry-like fruits, which only appear in suitable weather conditions.

Flowers are cup-shaped and approximately 12mm (½in) across and long lasting. The shrub can be grown successfully on a wide variety of soils and will tolerate chalky soils better than the common laurel. It can also be grown as a tree on a single stem, forming an attractive evergreen tree with the added attraction of the display of flowers.

Weigela florida 'Variegata' AGM
Family: Caprifoliaceae

A deciduous shrub producing leaves and sometimes flowers as early as April. *W. florida* originates from Asia, including China and Japan.

Left un-pruned, this shrub will easily grow to 2.5m (8ft). Its leaves are opposite, ovate and tapering to a point, approximately 10–12cm (4–5in) long with cream or grey prominent markings and remain on the shrub until the first frosts of autumn. Five-lobed and dark-pink flowers, approximately 2cm (1in) long, form over a long period of many weeks.

These flowers are produced in short clusters, on stems produced the previous year or older branches. The shrub tolerates a wide variety of soils in a sunny or partly shaded position. Prune to remove older wood that bears fewer flowers and to encourage strong new shoots from ground level, otherwise the shrub can become 'leggy'.

Varieties & Forms

WEIGELA FLORIDA 'FOLIIS PURPUREIS' AGM Has dark-red and purple-coloured leaves. Usually more compact, growing to 1.5m (5ft).

WEIGELA MIDDENDORFIANA A more compact shrub with large leaves and hairy undersides. Bears creamy yellow flowers, with orange markings on the throat, up to 4cm (1½in) long, flowering in July.

Allium karataviense AGM

A bulbous plant originating from Asia and normally found growing among broken limestone rock.

From large bulbs, the plant produces two thick leathery grey-green lance-shaped leaves in early spring. These leaves are up to 30cm (12in) long and grow close to the soil surface. As the bulbs age, the leaf dimensions increase and may be up to 7.5cm (3in) wide. From the centre of each pair of leaves an umbel grows, composed of up to 60 small pink, star-shaped flowers approximately 8mm (½in) across. Each umbel may be 7–10cm (3–4in) across.

As the flowers open, the stem carries on extending until reaching a height of 25cm (10in). Flower buds may sometimes be damaged by late spring frosts. Slugs and snails may also be a problem. Grow in full sun in a well-draining fertile soil. Improve drainage by adding coarse grit or a surface mulch of decorative chippings. There are numerous species and varieties of allium, but none have the appearance of *A. karataviense*.

Buddleja alternifolia AGM
Family: Buddlejaceae

Originating from China, this deciduous species forms a large shrub or, if trained on one stem, a small tree, which can grow up to 4m (13ft) high. Introduced into the UK nearly 100 years ago by Reginald Farrer.

Long arching stems produce alternate leaves up to 7cm (3in) long, they are dark green, sometimes silvery beneath. In late spring and early summer, the branches are covered in numerous clusters of fragrant pale-purple flowers. The clusters are 3–5cm (1½–2in) across.

As flowers are produced on the previous year's growth, careful pruning needs to be carried out to ensure a balance of different aged branches. Grow in a fertile soil in a sunny situation. Can also be effectively grown against a wall or a fence.

Kalmia latifolia AGM

Family: Ericaceae Common name: Icing Sugar or Calico Bush

An evergreen shrub, found growing wild on mountains in the eastern states of the USA, from Maine to Florida.

Fairly slow growing, this shrub will eventually grow to 3m (10ft). Its rather brittle branches carry alternate oval-shaped, shiny, dark-green leaves up to 12cm (5in) long. During April and May, large clusters of distinctly shaped flower buds are formed. They are dark pink and resemble iced cake decorations, opening to cup-shaped flowers up to 2.5cm (1in) across.

This plant requires an acid soil, moisture retentive but free draining, preferring light shade. Top dress annually with leaf mould or similar organic material. Prune only to remove older flowered stems or dead branches.

Varieties & Forms

KALMIA LATIFOLIA 'ELF'
Compact, only growing to 1.2m (4ft) with smaller leaves and white flowers.

KALMIA LATIFOLIA 'BULLSEYE'
Has white flowers with striking red stripes on the inside.

KALMIA LATIFOLIA 'OSTBO RED'
AGM Bright-red buds open to reveal pink flowers.

Prostanthera cuneata AGM

Family: Labiatae Common name: Alpine Mint Bush

From the mountains of New South Wales and Tasmania in Australia, this is one of many species becoming more popular in the United Kingdom. *P. cuneata* is the hardiest, but is still borderline and would need some protection in severe winters.

Strongly aromatic and growing up to 95cm (36in) high, *P. Cuneata* forms a very bushy plant with greenish stems and small, almost round dark-green and strongly aromatic leaves, approximately 7mm (¼in) across. In cold weather the plant will become semi-evergreen (almost deciduous). Over a long period of time, the shrub is covered with white flowers with uneven lips, up to 2cm (1in) across. They have mauve and yellow markings on the lower petals.

Prefers a sunny position in a fertile well-draining soil. It will not tolerate an exposed position, where cold winds will adversely affect it. Trim after flowering to keep compact, but do not cut back into older wood, as new growth buds will not develop.

There are many other species of Prostanthera but none are reliably hardy, so they have not been detailed here.

Iris orientalis

Family: Iridaceae Common name: Oriental Iris

Growing wild in northern Greece and western Turkey, it can also be found on the Greek Islands of Lesbos and Samos, where it grows in damp meadows and marshes at altitudes of up to 1500m (4700ft).

Growing from a rhizomatous clump, flowering stems are produced in mid-May to mid-June, growing to a height of 80 to 90cm (36in). Large very attractive flowers up to 10cm (4in) across are mainly white with yellow blotches on the fall petals. A variety 'Shelford Giant' was discovered near Ephesus in Turkey and, as the name suggests, it grows much taller and has larger flowers.

Needs to be grown in a moisture-retentive soil or grown on the margin of a pond. This plant takes a few years to settle into a new position before it will produce its beautiful flowers.

Varieties & Forms

IRIS ORIENTALIS 'SHELFORD GIANT' Flowers are lemon yellow up to 12cm (5in) across and the plant can grow up to 1.8m (6ft).

Clematis alpina AGM

Family: Ranunculaceae Common name: Alpine Clematis

Found growing in mountainous areas of southern Europe, flowering in spring over a long period. Photograph taken at Cranborne Manor garden in Dorset.

Twining stems clinging to supports using the leaf petioles will grow to a maximum of 3m (10ft). Leaves are composed of three mid-green leaflets, approximately 5cm (2in) long. Flowers are produced on the previous year's growth, up to 6cm (3in) across. Bell-shaped flowers are composed of four blue tepals and white centres, usually nodding. Attractive feathery seed heads persist after flowering. Sometimes a second period of flowering occurs in the autumn.

Grow in well-drained soil in a sunny position. Prune after flowering to remove dead or broken stems and to shorten long growths, to keep it within its allocated space.

Varieties & Forms

CLEMATIS ALPINA FORM ALBA
Slow growing with creamy-white flowers.

CLEMATIS ALPINA 'PINK FLAMINGO' Has semi-double pale-pink flowers for a long period of time.

Philadelphus x burfordensis
Family: Hydrangeaceae
Common name: Mock Orange Blossom

Not occurring in the wild, this shrub was first found growing at Burford Court in Surrey.

Deciduous shrub grown for its very fragrant flowers in early summer. It is upright growing, producing vigorous new shoots up to 3m (10ft) long. It has dark-green oval-shaped leaves up to 12cm (5in) long, produced in pairs with long internodes. Clusters of white cup-shaped, fragrant flowers 5–7cm (2–3in) across are borne in small racemes of up to 10 flowers on growth that is one year or older.

Grows well in most soils, preferably in full sun. Prune after flowering to remove old growth and to shorten very vigorous stems.

Varieties & Forms

PHILADELPHUS 'BELLE ETOILE' AGM Has a delicious orange blossom fragrance with white flowers that have a purplish centre, carried on 1.5m (5ft) high plants.

PHILADELPHUS 'SYBILLE' AGM Suitable for the smaller garden, only growing to 1m (3ft), with fragrant white flowers.

Buddleja globosa AGM
Family: Buddlejaceae Common name: Orange Ball Tree

Originating from South America, including the countries of Chile and Argentina.

A vigorous, stiff, upright-growing, semi-evergreen shrub, growing up to 5m (16ft) high. Depending upon weather conditions during the winter months, the leaves may be retained. The leaves are dark green and lance-shaped up to 20cm (8in) long, with woolly undersides. Rounded clusters of fragrant orange and yellow flowers approximately 5cm (2in) across are formed in panicles of up to 10 flowers in June and July.

Young shoots can be damaged by severe frosts in some winters. Grow in full sun in fertile soil. Minimal pruning is needed, only being necessary to remove old flowered stems and finished flower heads in order to keep the shrub tidy.

Varieties & Forms

BUDDLEJA x WEYERIANA A hybrid formed by the crossing of *B. davidii* and *B globosa*, exhibiting some of the characters of both parents.

Lamium maculatum 'Sterling Silver'
Family: Labiatae Common name: Dead Nettle

The species *L. maculatum* grows wild in North Africa and Europe, including the United Kingdom.

Typical of Labiates, this plant has square stems and oval coarsely toothed opposite leaves up to 6cm (2½in) long. They are silver with pale green undersides, turning darker as the summer turns to autumn. Whorls of two lipped pale-purple flowers are produced in the leaf axils over a long period of weeks starting in early May.

Stems grow up to 20cm (8in) tall, spreading to provide valuable ground cover forming large clumps up to 75cm (30in) across.

This plant is tolerant of a wide variety of soil types and will grow in full sun or partial shade, although the denser the shade, the less the plant will flower and its leaves will not be as well marked with silver. In damp shady conditions, the plant's foliage may be damaged by slugs and snails. Trim annually to restrict the plant spreading.

Varieties & Forms

LAMIUM MACULATUM F ALBUM
Has green leaves with silver margins.

LAMIUM MACULATUM 'WHITE NANCY' AGM This plant has silver leaves edged green, growing 15cm (6in) high with clusters of pure-white flowers.

Erigeron glaucus 'Elstead Pink'

Family: Asteraceae Common name: Beach Aster

This species originates from the west coast of the USA. As this is the first member of the Daisy (*Asteraceae*) family featured, it may be worth noting that all members of this family have flower heads composed of hundreds of individual flowers.

Creeping fleshy stems form large spreading plants up to 45cm (18in) across, bearing more or less spoon-shaped leaves 10–12cm (4–5in) long. The flowers have golden-yellow central disc florets, surrounded by lilac/pink ray florets. Overall, the flower head is approximately 5cm (2in) across.

Plant in fertile soil that does not dry out in the summer. Dead-head regularly in order to prolong the flowering period, which may continue for many weeks.

Varieties & Forms

ERIGERON 'DUNKELSTE ALLER' AGM Taller, growing up to 60cm (24in), having long dark-violet/blue ray florets, with a contrasting yellow centre.

ERIGERON 'QUAKERESS' A vigorous clump-forming plant with large numbers of flower heads. The pale-pink ray florets are produced over a long period.

Deutzia longifolia 'Veitchii'
Family: Saxifragaceae

A deciduous shrub found growing in China, the slightly arching stems grow up to 2m (6ft). New stems are produced each year from below ground and produce flowers from the second year on.

The leaves are narrow, lance-shaped and up to 10cm (4in) long. Numerous flowers grow in panicles up to 8cm (3in) long, formed of 15 to 20 flowers. Individual flowers up to 2cm (1in) across, are star shaped and pale pink with white edges to the petals flowering in June and July.

Position in full sun, in a fertile moisture-retentive soil. Prune after flowering to remove older flowered 'canes', leaving new stems to produce the most flowers.

Varieties & Forms

DEUTZIA SCABRA Taller, with numerous white fragrant flowers.

DEUTZIA GRACILIS A compact shrub growing to approximately 1m (3ft) with fragrant white flowers.

Hypericum 'Hidcote' AGM
Family: Clusiaceae Common name: St John's Wort

A hybrid of garden origin, taking its name form the famous garden at Hidcote Manor in Gloucestershire.

Growing to a height of 1.2m (4ft) this shrub is usually evergreen, depending upon position and winter weather, which can render it semi-evergreen. Its leaves are narrow, dark green and lance-shaped, growing to 5–7cm (2–3in) long. In summer it produces clusters of large single bright-yellow flowers up to 7cm (3in) across, with a distinctive tuft of golden-yellow stamens.

Flowers are produced over several weeks. Often, this shrub has a second flowering period in August or September. Plant in fertile soil in a sunny position.

Varieties & Forms

HYPERICUM x INODORUM 'ELSTEAD' Has smaller leaves and large clusters of small flowers, up to 3cm (1¼in) across followed by attractive pinkish-red seed capsules, which are useful for flower arranging.

HYPERICUM PATULUM A similar-looking plant with slightly smaller flowers produced in larger numbers.

HYPERICUM FRONDOSUM A deciduous shrub, flowering in late summer, its yellow flowers have a very large golden central tuft of stamens.

Astrantia maxima

Family: Umbelliferae Common name: Hattie's Pincushion

Flowering in July and August, this herbaceous tufted perennial originates from Eastern Europe and parts of Asia, growing in hillside meadows and woodland edges.

The leaves form close mats and grow up to 30cm (12in) high, each leaf composed of three lobes, which are toothed and up to 10cm (4in) across. Flower heads are composed of numerous pink flowers, surrounded by up to 12 pink bracteoles, giving the appearance of sharply pointed petals. The flower heads are up to 5cm (2in) across and grow to a height of 45cm (18in).

Preferring a damp moisture-retentive soil, the plant is generally pest and disease free, although aphids can be a nuisance towards the end of the flowering period.

Varieties & Forms

ASTRANTIA MAJOR 'RUBRA'
Dark-red flower heads, on branched stems, growing vigorously up to 90cm (36in)

ASTRANTIA 'SUNNINGDALE VARIEGATED' AGM With pale pink flower heads set off by creamy-white margined leaves.

Santolina rosmarinifolia
Family: Asteraceae

Found in the wild in the countries of the Mediterranean, including Portugal, Spain and France.

A compact mound-forming evergreen shrub growing up to 75cm (30in) high. Its leaves are light green, aromatic and finely divided, growing up to 5cm (2in) long. Flowering stems stand clear of the densely crowded foliage topped by bright-yellow flower heads up to 3cm (1¼in) across. Flowering usually occurs in June and July.

Requires a quick-draining soil to grow well. To keep the shrub tidy, clip with shears immediately after the flowers have finished. This shrub may be damaged by very cold, snowy winters.

Varieties & Forms

SANTOLINA ROSMARINIFOLIA 'PRIMROSE GEM' AGM This variety has pale-yellow flower heads.

Lychnis coronaria

Family: Caryophyllaceae Common name: Rose Campion

A native of Southern Europe, including Greece, the former Yugoslavia and Northern Italy, this plant can also be found in Northern Africa growing in dry rocky areas.

An erect, clump-forming, short-living perennial; this plant can be treated as a biennial, as it produces vast quantities of seed. Because of this, the flowers should be removed when they are finished, otherwise hundreds of seedlings will be produced throughout the garden.

The whole plant is woolly, giving the appearance of having silver leaves and stems. Its leaves are lance-shaped, with basal leaves being up to 20cm (8in) long and leaves on the flowering stems up to 9cm (4in) long.

Flowers are produced from June to September, the flowering period being extended if flowers are removed as they fade. They are reddish purple, up to 3cm (1¼in) across, and the petals are slightly reflexed. Flowers are arranged in cymes but open individually, extending the flowering period. Plants eventually reach a height of 90cm (36in) with a spread of approximately 40cm (16in).

This plant is not difficult to grow and will tolerate most of the soil types it encounters, flowering at its best on drier soils. Grow in a sunny position. Slugs and snails may be a problem early in the spring as the new basal leaves are emerging.

Varieties & Forms

LYCHNIS CORONARIA 'ALBA' AGM
Has white flowers (occasionally, white flowered seedlings will arise from
L. coronaria).

LYCHNIS CORONARIA 'ABBOTSWOOD ROSE' A beautiful pink-flowered form on compact plants.

Brachyglottis laxifolia

Family: Asteraceae Common name: New Zealand Daisy Bush

This plant is a native of New Zealand, where it is found growing wild on the South Island.

A straggling, spreading evergreen shrub that is attractive throughout the year. It has elliptic dark-green leaves with silvery hairy undersides up to 5cm (2in) long. The silvery hairs also cover buds, giving a general silvered appearance that enhances the yellow daisy flowers. Yellow flower heads measuring up to 3cm (1½in) across are carried in large lax panicles throughout the summer to early autumn.

The shrub will grow to 1.2m (4ft) high, but with a much greater spread due to its growth habit. Flowers best in a sunny position in freely draining soil. Pruning is only required to keep it tidy and within its allotted space. May be damaged by very cold, frosty weather.

Varieties & Forms

BRACHYGLOTTIS DUNEDIN HYBRIDS These are generally widely available, particularly 'Sunshine' AGM.

Crocosmia 'Lucifer' AGM

Family: Iridaceae Common name: Montbretia

This cultivar is one of many hybrids developed from Crocosmia species from South Africa. Raised by Blooms of Bressingham, this is one of several introductions originating from that famous nursery.

Growing from underground corms, the stems grow rapidly in late spring and early summer, producing quantities of dark-green pleated, lance-shaped leaves, up to 60cm (24in) long. The stems grow to 1.15m (3½ft) and are topped with upward-facing funnel-shaped bright scarlet flowers, up to 5cm (2in) long in many-flowered spikes, throughout July and August.

Due to the often-heavy flower heads it is best to support stems with twiggy branches or canes early in the season to prevent the stems from collapsing when wet or being blown in the wind. Lift and divide clumps that have become overcrowded and are losing vigour. These plants do best in full sun, but will tolerate some light shade and are generally pest and disease free.

Varieties & Forms

CROCOSMIA 'FIREBIRD' This is shorter than 'Lucifer', growing up to 80cm (32in), with orange-red flowers

CROCOSMIA 'STAR OF THE EAST' Has large orange flowers with a paler centre, growing to 70cm (28in).

CROCOSMIA 'GOLDEN FLEECE' This produces large numbers of pale yellow flowers on stems up to 60cm (24in) in late summer.

Hydrangea quercifolia AGM
Family: Hydrangeaceae
Common name: Oak-leaved Hydrangea

Originating from the Eastern states of the USA as far south as Florida and flowering in early summer.

Usually flowering in July and August in the United Kingdom, this shrub is deciduous, growing up to 2m (6ft) high. It can have a very untidy growth habit, with angular and spreading branches. Its leaves are coarsely hairy, with a shape reminiscent of large oak leaves, approximately 15cm (6in) long and 10cm (4in) wide. They change colour in the autumn, turning a reddish bronze before they fall.

The shrub produces numerous crowded panicles of sterile and normal flowers up to 20cm (8in) across, lasting for several weeks. Individual sterile white flowers are up to 4cm (1½in) across. As the sterile flowers age, they become tinged with red or purple.

Well-drained soil is best for successful growth, but it will also benefit from an annual mulch of garden compost or leaf mould. Full sun is ideal, but light shade is also tolerated.

Varieties & Forms

HYDRANGEA QUERCIFOLIA 'SNOW FLAKE' This variety has large drooping panicles of double creamy-white flowers, lasting for several weeks before they turn pink.

Echinacea purpurea
Family: Asteraceae Common name: Cone Flower

This plant commonly grows wild in many of the states of the USA on dry prairies. Flowering occurs over a long period of many weeks from July to late September.

Branched flowering stems grow up to 1.4m (4½ft) and bear slightly hairy, oval mid-green leaves up to 12cm (5in) long in opposite pairs. Flower heads are up to 12cm (5in) across and are composed of a central cone of brown disc florets with golden stamens. The flower's outer ray florets are dark pink and slightly reflexed.

Well-draining soil, preferably in full sun, is the preferred location. Remove flowers as they fade to prolong the flowering period.

Varieties & Forms

ECHINACEA 'ROBERT BLOOM' This variety has lilac-purple flowers and was raised by Blooms of Bressingham.

ECHINACEA 'WHITE LUSTRE' Grows to a height of 75cm (30in) and has white ray florets and an array of beautiful golden disc stamens.

Phlox paniculata
Family: Polemoniacceae

Hybrids of this plant were introduced from the USA in the 18th century and numerous named cultivars have been raised over the years. Many cultivars have a subtle fragrance, which is more obvious in the evening.

This herbaceous perennial plant produces stiffly erect stems from a creeping rootstock. The stems grow up to 1.2m (4ft), bearing light-green, narrowly pointed leaves up to 10cm (4in) long that are arranged in opposite pairs. Flowers are salverform, each up to 3cm (1¼in) across and arranged in dense panicles approximately 20cm (8in) in diameter. The leaves die quickly, giving the plants an untidy appearance in the late autumn.

Grow in full sun in a fertile well-draining soil. Do not allow the plant to dry out, as this encourages the onset of mildew, which can be very damaging as it reduces the vigour and flowering capability of this plant. Slugs and snails may cause damage to newly emerging growths. Remove flowers as they fade to extend the flowering period over a period of several weeks.

Divide the rootstock and replant the newer shoots every four or five years, discarding the older parts that flower less.

Varieties & Forms

PHLOX PANICULATA 'FUJIYAMA' AGM Up to 75cm (30in) with large flower heads of pure-white flowers.

PHLOX PANICULATA 'NORAH LEIGH' This plant has ivory variegated leaves and small pale lilac-pink flowers with a darker-pink eye.

PHLOX PANICULATA 'STARFIRE' Deep-red flowers (illustrated above) with dark-green leaves, up to 75cm (30in) tall.

Hibiscus syriacus
Family: Malvaceae

Very few hibiscus are reliably hardy in the United Kingdom, but this species from Asia is hardy in most regions of the country.

A large shrub or a small tree, but usually grown as a shrub; in other European countries it is often grown as a street tree. Its dark-green leaves are usually oval-shaped and up to 10cm (4in) long. Flowers are produced over a long period from late summer; they are pink trumpet-shaped flowers with crinkled petals, up to 7cm (3in) across, featuring yellow anthers. Sometimes, the centre of the flower is streaked a dark-red colour. This shrub grows rather untidily but it will eventually reach a height of 3.5m (12ft).

Prune in spring just before new growth commences to remove any dead stems and shorten any straggly or untidy growth.

Varieties & Forms

HIBISCUS SYRIACUS 'RED HEART' AGM Has beautiful white flowers with dark-red markings at the base of the trumpet (right).

HIBISCUS SYRIACUS 'BLUE BIRD' Has violet-blue flowers up to 7cm (3in) across with red markings.

HIBISCUS SYRIACUS 'PINK GIANT' AGM This plant's large dark-pink flowers have dark-red central markings.

Hebe salicifolia
Family: Scrophulariaceae

As with the majority of species of hebe, this plant originates from New Zealand.

A tall spreading evergreen shrub, growing up to 2.4m (8ft) high. Its narrowly pointed mid-green leaves are approximately 10cm (4in) long. Racemes of small pale-lilac or white flowers up to 15cm (6in) long form during the late summer and autumn, sometimes continuing into the early winter.

Frosty weather can cause some defoliation. Hebes will grow and flower well in poor soil, but the soil does need to be moist but well-drained. This plant prefers full sun for maximum flowering. Provide shelter from cold drying winds in bad weather in order to prevent leaf loss. In some seasons, aphids may be a problem as they may attack flower clusters and terminal buds. Capsids (pests) may also cause some leaf distortion.

Varieties & Forms

HEBE 'GAUNTLETTII' Growing to 1m (40in) with glossy dark-green leaves and pendent racemes of pinkish-purple from up to 15cm (6in) long.

HEBE 'MIDSUMMER BEAUTY' AGM Up to 2m (6ft) tall with 18cm (7in) long pointed racemes of small pale-violet flowers. This hebe flowers for several months.

Geranium pratense 'Plenum Violaceum' AGM

Family: Geraniaceae

This form of *G. pratense* is very different from the common species that originates from Asia, including China.

The leaves arise from a compact rootstock with thick fleshy roots. Basal leaves are approximately 10cm (4in) across with petioles up to 45cm (18in) long. Flowering stems produced in the summer grow up to 90cm (3ft) and have numerous branches bearing large numbers of flowers. The plant may have a spread of 90–120cm (36–48in) across.

The flowers are fully double, approximately 2–4cm (1–2in) in diameter, coloured deep purple with a reddish tinge. As with many of the taller varieties, it has weak stems that can be easily damaged by heavy rain or strong winds, so it is best if supports are put in place early as the stems grow. Plant in fertile soil and to prevent attacks of mildew, water in dry periods.

Varieties & Forms

GERANIUM PRATENSE 'MRS KENDALL CLARK' AGM Has pale-blue single flowers with pinkish stripes.

GERANIUM PRATENSE 'PLENUM ALBUM' The double white flowers have a violet tinge.

Liatris spicata
Family: Asteraceae Common name: Gayfeather

Originating from the eastern states of the US and favouring damp ground conditions, this plant flowers in summer and early autumn, growing from short underground rhizomes covered in papery scales.

The plant varies in height from 70cm to 1m (28–40in) producing stiff upright stems from a basal cluster of narrow linear leaves up to 40cm (16in) long. Flowering commences at the tip of the spike downwards, forming pale purple or white spikes and may eventually extend to 25cm (10in). Individual flowers are composed of numerous ray florets having narrow and curled-in petals.

If the soil is too wet, the rootstock can rot in cold winter conditions, but, in the summer, a moisture-retentive soil is required. Slugs and snails can cause severe damage to young emerging foliage and stems. This is a very useful plant for providing cut flowers.

Varieties & Forms

LIATRIS SPICATA 'KOBOLD' This plant has deep-purple flowers on short stems up to 50cm (20in) long.

LIATRIS SPICATA 'SNOW QUEEN' White flower spikes on stems up to 70cm (28in).

Helianthus x multiflorus
Family: Asteraceae Common name: Sunflower

A hybrid plant of garden origin, probably having *H. annuus* and *H. decapetalus* as the parents. There are many selections of this plant and some have double flowers.

A quickly growing, clump-forming herbaceous perennial producing flowering stems up to 2m (6ft). Its slender stems are sparsely covered with dark-green lance-shaped leaves up to 18cm (7in) long. Flower heads formed of central brownish disc florets and colourful golden-yellow ray florets up to 12cm (5in) across.

In exposed positions the plant may require support to prevent damage to the flowering stems. Grow in full sun. The plant will tolerate dry conditions but produces better flowers in moisture-retentive soil. Slugs and snails may damage young shoots and mildew may be a problem in drought conditions.

Varieties & Forms

HELIANTHUS x MULTIFLORUS 'CAPENNOCH STAR' AGM Grows to 1.5m (5ft) and is good for cutting, having lemon-yellow ray florets and dark-yellow central disc florets.

HELIANTHUS x MULTIFLORUS 'LODDON GOLD' AGM Has fully double golden-yellow flower heads.

Thalictrum delavayi AGM
Family: Ranunculaceae Common name: Meadow Rue

Found growing in high mountains in Southern China where it flowers during the summer months.

A tall-growing, sometimes untidy plant, it is effective if allowed to grow through other smaller early flowering perennials. Its very dark-green stems grow up to 1.2m (4ft) and will need canes or twigs if other plants are not around to support it. Leaves are composed of three leaflets on very long petioles, 8–12cm (4–5in) long. Flowers up to 2cm (¾in) across, are produced on long stalks over a lengthy period of time. They have pink or lilac narrow sepals and long yellow stamens, giving a feathery appearance.

Grow in fertile moisture-retentive soil with light shade if possible, this can be provided by planting amongst other lower-growing shrubs. Growth commences late in the year. Slugs and snails may be a problem in damp conditions. Divide regularly every three or four years to maintain the plant's vigour.

Varieties & Forms

THALICTRUM DELAVAYI 'ALBUM'
This variety has white sepals with golden-yellow stamens.

THALICTRUM DELAVAYI 'HEWITT'S DOUBLE' AGM This plant has no stamens but numerous pink sepals, forming fully double fluffy flowers in large open panicles.

Monarda 'Violet Queen'
Family: Lamiaceae Common name: Bergamot

Originally found growing in the eastern states of USA, where *M. didyma* grows on dry prairies and along the edges of woodlands, flowering from July to September.

A clump-forming herbaceous perennial, producing stems up to 90cm (36in) tall. The square stems are occasionally branched and are topped with whorls of flowers produced in the leaf axils. Petals are tubular, violet-coloured, approximately 5cm (2in) long, emerging from reddish-coloured bracts. The aromatic leaves are mid- to dark-green with conspicuous veins and are up to 12cm (4½in) long.

This plant grows best in full sun, but will tolerate some light shade. A moisture-retentive soil gives the best results, but it must be free draining. Slugs and snails may cause damage to newly emerging shoots in early spring. Mildew may also be a problem on some cultivars in hot dry conditions.

All varieties detailed were probably derived from *M.didyma*.

Varieties & Forms

MONARDA 'CAMBRIDGE SCARLET' AGM A long-established favourite nearly 100-years-old, proving a reliable variety flowering over a long period, having scarlet-red flowers.

MONARDA 'SCHNEEWITTCHEN' With white flowers emerging from green-coloured bracts.

MONARDA 'CROFTWAY PINK' AGM Has beautiful clear pink flowers and contrasting dark-pinkish bracts.

Alstroemeria psittacina

Family: Alstroemeriaceae Common name: Peruvian Lily

The origins of this exotic-looking flower are in Mexico and parts of South America, flowering in December and January.

Stems arise from a fleshy rootstock and grow up to 1m (3ft) high. Light-green oblong-shaped leaves approximately 10cm (4in) long are evenly spaced along the flowering stems. Flowers form in clusters and are reddish, streaked variably with chocolate, yellow and green. Growing up to 7cm (3in) long, they consist of six tepals, giving the plant a very exotic appearance.

A free-draining soil is needed to grow this plant, but the fleshy rootstock should not be allowed to dry out. Mulch regularly for the first few years after planting until it is well established, and protect the crown if severe frost is anticipated.

Slugs and snails may be a problem early in the growing season, attacking the soft new shoots.

Varieties & Forms

ALSTROEMERIA HOOKERI A low-growing species up to 50cm (20in), with large pink flowers.

ALSTROEMERIA LIGTU HYBRIDS, Commonly available, variable seedlings with bicolour flowers of yellow, with either white, orange or red.

Sternbergia lutea

Family: Amaryllidaceae Common name: Autumn Daffodil

This bulbous plant originates from Southern Europe and also from the mountains of Turkey and Afghanistan.

Although only suitable for the mildler counties of the United Kingdom, this autumn-flowering bulb will produce large numbers of crocus- like goblet-shaped deep-yellow flowers up to 3cm (1¼in) across. Flowers form at the same time as the emerging leaves, which are narrow, dark green and up to 25cm (10in) long, as they continue growing after flowering has finished.

Grow in a sunny sheltered position in well-draining fertile soil. This bulbous plant is affected by the same virus diseases that are common among narcissus. This can cause streaking and distorted leaves and a reduction of flowers. Narcissus flies may also damage the bulbs, causing them to rot. Suitable for planting in pots or other containers that can be moved inside if long cold and frosty conditions prevail.

Varieties & Forms

STERNBERGIA CANDIDA Its fragrant white funnel-shaped flowers are produced in late winter.

STERNBERGIA CLUSIANA Golden-yellow flowers, up to 10cm (4in) high are produced in autumn before the narrow grey-green leaves arrive.

Ceratostigma willmottianum
Family: Plumbaginaceae

This plant is found in the wild in western China, flowering from August to October.

A deciduous shrub with thin wiry stems, growing to 1m (40in). It has small mid-green leaves up to 5cm (2in) long, with reddish margins and reddish petioles. The flowers, produced in axillary clusters, are salverform, pale blue with a paler centre and up to 3cm (1¼in) across. The flower tubes and calyces are reddish, which adds to this plant's appeal.

May sometimes be damaged by hard frosts, but will usually recover. Grow in fertile, light and well-draining soil. To keep the shrub tidy and to maintain good flowering, prune after petals fall to remove all flowered stems.

Varieties & Forms

CERATOSTIGMA PLUMBAGINOIDES AGM Smaller in height, up to 45cm (18in) and having darker-blue flowers. Grows from suckering stems.

Kirengeshoma palmatum AGM
Family: Hydrangeaceae

Originating from Japan, growing in woodlands on hillsides, where it flowers from August to September.

A woody perennial growing from a thick underground rhizome. Its spreading stems grow quickly and attain a height of 1.2m (4ft) in good conditions. The leaves are slightly hairy, mid green and palmately shaped, up to 20cm (8in) long. Flowers are produced in August and early September, they are pale-yellow and formed in few-flowered cymes. The slightly tubular flowers have fleshy petals up to 3cm (1¼in) long, with slightly recurved lobes.

This plant prefers moist soil, top dressed annually with leaf mould or well-rotted garden compost. An acid soil in slight shade is ideal and the plant needs to be sheltered from cold drying winds. Slugs and snails are often a problem as they eat the new shoots and flowers. There are only two species of this perennial and usually only this species is available.

Eucryphia glutinosa AGM
Family: Eucryphiaceae

An evergreen tree usually found growing in moist woodlands in southern Chile. *E. lucida* originates from Australia.

Although it is fairly slow growing, this tree will attain a height of 10m (33ft) in sheltered situations. It is excellent as a specimen tree in a lawn, allowing it to develop its full potential. Usually evergreen but may lose leaves in very cold, frosty weather. The plant's pinnate leaves are glossy, dark green and prominently toothed, composed of three or five leaflets, measuring up to 6cm (2½in) long.

During summer and early autumn, beautiful cup-shaped white flowers with four large petals are produced, up to 6cm (2½in) across. The centre of the flower has a distinctive cluster of numerous golden-yellow stamens. Can be allowed to develop as a large shrub without a trunk. A neutral or acid soil is preferred, which should be moist but not waterlogged. Keep the roots cool and in the shade, with the crown in full sun.

Varieties & Forms

EUCRYPHIA x NYMANSENSIS 'NYMANSAY' AGM Raised at Nyman's Garden, Sussex, this hybrid will tolerate a slightly alkaline soil. Its flowers and leaves are larger than *E. glutinosa*.

EUCRYPHIA LUCIDA 'PINK CLOUD' Slightly more tender, only being suitable for the mildest areas in a sheltered situation. It has narrow leaves and pink flowers with darker centres.

Galtonia candicans

Family: Hyacinthaceae Common name: Summer Hyacinth

A small genus of bulbous plants, originating from South Africa, where it is common in grassland locations.

Leaves appear in late spring from the large bulbs. They are slightly fleshy, greyish-green and lance-shaped, growing up to 5cm (2in) wide and approximately 60cm (24in) long. The flower stems grow rapidly to 65cm (26in) tall, carrying up to 35 white tubular and pendent flowers. The flowers have green markings on the white petals and are up to 4cm (1½in) long.

Grow in a sunny position in a fertile moisture-retentive soil. If grown in areas prone to prolonged frosty periods, it is best to lift the bulbs and replant in the early spring. Slugs and snails may be troublesome during a wet season, damaging emerging leaves and flower stems.

Varieties & Forms

GALTONIA VIRIDIFLORA AGM
Less tall and its flowering stems have approximately 30 tubular hanging greenish flowers. Not as hardy as *G. candicans.*

Hydrangea arborescens 'Grandiflora' AGM

Family: Hydrangeaceae

This plant originates from the eastern states of the USA, growing in woodlands and on shady mountain sides.

A fairly vigorous deciduous shrub, producing long new shoots annually. These shoots grow up to 1.8m (6ft) high and are topped with large rounded heads of numerous greenish-white, mainly fertile flowers. These heads may be 20cm (8in) or more across and may become weighed down following heavy rain. The plant's opposite leaves are mid-green, prominently veined and up to 18cm (7in) long. Flower heads persist well after the leaves fall and are ideal for using in flower arrangements.

Grow in moist fertile soils in light shade. Prune in spring, removing long flowered stems back to the main branch framework. An application of organic fertiliser in spring can be beneficial.

Varieties & Forms

HYDRANGEA ARBORESCENS 'ANNABELLE' AGM Has very large flowerheads that are composed mainly of sterile flowers.

Eucomis 'Sparkling Burgundy'

Family: Hyacinthaceae Common name: Pineapple Lily

Bulbous perennials originating from South Africa and the mountains of other southern African countries.

This particular striking cultivar is a fairly recent introduction. Large bulbs produce a basal rosette of linear, strap-shaped leaves up to 40cm (16in) long and approximately 5cm (2in) wide. The leaves and stems are purplish red, the former with a distinct paler central midrib. Flowering stems grow up to 50cm (20in) or occasionally more and carry numerous star-shaped flowers up to 2cm across.

Flowers are purple in bud opening to pale pink and composed of six tepals, distinctly pale-purple ovaries and greenish stamens. They last for several weeks, sometimes until the first frost. Some protection is required to shelter the bulbs from severe frosts and the newly emerging foliage can also be damaged by frosts, along with wet weather or slugs and snails. Grow in a sunny well-draining soil, sheltered by a wall or a fence.

Varieties & Forms

EUCOMIS BICOLOR Stems marked with reddish flecks carry greenish flowers, the tepals have maroon margins, all topped with a tuft of green leaves.

EUCOMIS COMOSA Stems up to 75cm (30in) long carry a crowded spike of greenish-white flowers marked with purple, and purple ovaries.

Abelia x grandiflora
Family: Caprifoliaceae

A hybrid formed following the crossing of two Chinese species, *A. chinensis,* and *A. uniflora,* raised over a hundred years ago in Italy.

An evergreen vigorous shrub, growing to 2.5m (8ft), although many selections do not reach this height. The glossy green leaves are often tinged red, particularly in the winter. They are opposite, oval-shaped and up to 5cm (2in) long. Numerous panicles of tubular white flowers up to 2cm (1in) long open from pinkish flower buds, produced over a long flowering period.

Persistent reddish pink calyces often remain as an attractive feature after flowering has ceased. Quite often, these colourful calyces remain on the plant throughout the winter months.

Varieties & Forms

ABELIA FLORIBUNDA AGM With a similar growth habit, it is less hardy so is best grown against a wall; has pendent dark-pink tubular flowers up to 5cm (2in) long.

ABELIA CHINENSIS This plant has small, white, fragrant, funnel-shaped flowers up to 8mm (½in) long.

Silene schafta AGM
Family: Caryophyllaceae Common name: Catchfly

Originally from Asia, where it grows in the mountains of northern Iran, in rocky screes and crevices.

Flowering in late summer and autumn, it is suitable for the rock garden or the front of a sunny border. The plant has a neat, compact but spreading habit with flowering stems up to 30cm (12in) high. The bright magenta flowers are produced in profusion over several weeks; they have five notched petals up to 2.5cm (1in) across. The narrow leaves are light green and up to 2.5cm (1in) long.

Grow in fertile well-draining soil in a sunny situation. This plant may be susceptible to damage caused by slugs and snails in damp weather conditions.

Varieties & Forms

SILENE SCHAFTA 'SHELL PINK' Is similar, but with pale-pink flowers.

SILENE UNIFLORA 'FLORE PLENO' ('Double Sea Campion') A semi-evergreen creeping plant with double white flowers.

Campsis grandiflora
Family: Bignoniaceae
Common name: Chinese Trumpet Creeper

A very vigorous climbing vine originating from China, where it grows on hills and lower slopes of mountains.

Deciduous leaves up to 25cm (10in) long are well spaced along the vigorous twining stems. The leaves have six to nine pairs of leaflets, which are glossy dark green and approximately 5cm (2in) long with coarse-toothed margins. Stems will grow up to 6m (20ft) annually. Flowers produced in late summer and autumn are funnel-shaped in clusters of up to ten and are approximately 7.5cm (3in) long. The open flower has five lobes measuring up to 3cm (1¼in) across.

Grow in full sun to ripen branches and maximise flowers the following year. A moist soil should be well draining, do not provide any fertiliser, which would encourage growth at the expense of flowers. Do not plant in exposed positions where the buds will be damaged by cold drying winds.

Varieties & Forms

CAMPSIS RADICANS 'FLAVA'
This yellow-flowered form is sometimes available.

Sedum spectabile AGM

Family: Crassulaceae Common name: Ice Plant

This perennial originates from China and Korea.

A fleshy leaved, clump-forming hardy perennial. Flowering stems are unbranched, growing up to 45cm (18in), topped with flat cymes (see glossary) of numerous star-shaped flowers up to 15cm (6in) across. The fleshy leaves are oval-shaped, greyish-green coloured and have scalloped edges, up to 7.5cm (3in) long. Dying flower stems become woody and will over-winter with a basal cluster of small shoots that is susceptible to damage from slugs and snails.

Grow in fertile well-draining soil, and divide every few years to maintain vigour. Flowering stems may become top-heavy and need support to stop damage to the flowering stems. Vine weevils and root rot may cause some damage.

Varieties & Forms

SEDUM 'RUBY GLOW' AGM Red stems and leaves, dark-red flowers.

SEDUM SPECTABILIS 'ICEBERG' With pale-green leaves and white flowers growing up to 40cm (16in) high.

SEDUM TELEPHIUM MAXIMUM 'ATROPURPUREUM' AGM This variety of a similar species has purple stems and leaves with smaller flower heads, growing up to 60cm (24in) high.

Tricyrtis formosana AGM

Family: Liliaceae
Common name: Toad Lily

This plant is found growing in the wild in Taiwan, where it favours shady forests, flowering in August and September.

Spreading by underground stolons, the stems will grow to a height of 90cm (36in). Flowers form in the upper leaf axils and also as a terminal cyme of each stem.

Flowers measure up to 3cm (1¼in) across and are composed of six tepals, star-shaped pink or white and heavily spotted with purple markings. Prominent stigmas are also heavily spotted and streaked with purple or dark red. The leaves are glossy and dark green with very prominent veins, up to 13cm (5in) long, with the uppermost leaves clasping the stem.

Grow in moist well-draining soil in light shade. Mulch annually with leaf mould or well-rotted garden compost. Slugs and snails may be a problem as the new shoots appear.

Varieties & Forms

TRICYRTIS HIRTA A similar plant, but with hairy leaves and the flowers have less spotting. This species is the one most often available in nurseries and garden centres.

TRICYRTIS 'LILAC TOWERS' Only growing to 60cm (24in), it has white flowers with lilac and purple spotting.

TRICYRTIS 'WHITE TOWERS' This plant has hairy leaves and white flowers that are produced in the leaf axils.

Clematis tangutica

Family: Ranunculaceae Common name: Lemon Peel Clematis

A native of central Asia, including China and southern Russia, often found scrambling through vegetation along river valleys in the high mountains.

A summer-flowering climbing plant (although it occasionally commences in spring in mild climates) that often continues into the early autumn. Vigorous growth is made each year that may be up to 6m (20ft) long. The leaves are dark green and rough with hairs to assist with climbing. They are usually bipinnate and approximately 7cm (3in) long.

Long erect flower stalks each carry a single lantern-shaped flower. Each nodding flower is composed of four bright-yellow stiff sepals with reflexed tips and a central cluster of stamens and styles. As the sepals fall, the seed head forms, which is made of attractive silvery fluffy pom-poms. Grow in fertile soil in full sun and ensure that the soil has an adequate supply of organic matter to keep the roots cool and moist. Prune annually in the autumn to remove old flowered stems and to encourage new shoots.

Varieties & Forms

CLEMATIS 'BILL MACKENZIE' This has large numbers of yellow bell-shaped flowers, with red-brown stamens followed by feathery seed heads.

AUTUMN

This is the season where the cooling temperatures bring forth glorious displays of colourful foliage and autumn fruits bringing added interest to flowering plants.

Weeks 38-48

Autumn covers the period from September to November and generally in autumn, 'colour' in the garden or countryside refers to coloured foliage. However this period of the gardening calendar can be the most colourful due to a number of factors. Many plants have this time of year as their main flowering period and autumn is usually the season when many fruits and berries colour and ripen. The foliage of many shrubs and trees change from green to reds, orange or brown. And gloriously, some summer flowering plants carry on flowering into the autumn and some, after a brief rest, have a second burst of colour.

Although the aim of this book is to provide suggestions for 'flowers' for every week of the year, at this time make the most of plants providing bonus benefits. I often refer to these bonus plants in the modern marketing jargon as 'BOGOF' (buy one get one free) – you might even get 'two' free!

Some examples of these bonus plants include flowering trees, such as Sorbus commixta, that flower in spring and then provide colourful berries and coloured foliage in the autumn.

Escallonia 'Iveyi' AGM (plant 123) is evergreen, flowers over a long period and has lovely fragrance, providing extra value in the garden.

Arbutus unedo AGM

Family: Ericaceae Common name: Strawberry Tree

Small tree or large shrub found wild in southern Europe and countries of the Middle East.

The stems of the Strawberry Tree have a very attractive reddish brown flaking bark, most obvious on larger branches of mature plants, which may grow up to 8m (25ft). The evergreen leaves are tough and leathery, glossy, dark green and up to 10cm (4in) long.

Greenish-white pitcher-shaped flowers are produced in pendent clusters in September and October, followed by green, round, irregular fruits that remain on the plant for several months. Eventually in the following August and September the fruits swell and turn orange then red. Approximately 2cm (1in) across, these are much-loved by birds but rather tasteless. The scientific name is something of a joke, being translated as *un*, meaning one and *edo* to eat... 'one is enough'.

Varieties & Forms

ARBUTUS x ANDRACHNOIDES AGM Has larger clusters of whitish flowers throughout the winter months, but rarely produces fruits.

ARBUTUS UNEDO 'ELFIN KING' Smaller-growing, flowering and fruiting whilst still young.

Gaura lindheimeri AGM
Family: Onagraceae

Found in the wild growing in the southern Gulf states of the USA, where it flowers in August and September.

This tufted herbaceous perennial, forms a stiff-stemmed plant up to 1m (3ft) tall. The stems are covered with dark-green narrow leaves up to 7cm (3in) long, with a reddish tinge. Flowers form in racemes 40cm (16in) long at the top of the stems and open over a long period of several weeks. They look delicate and graceful with narrow pinkish-white petals and clusters of long white curved stamens, up to 2cm (1in) across, opening in the early hours of each day.

Grow in full sun in a sheltered position. Requiring a fertile well-draining soil, this plant is useful for hot dry situations.

Varieties & Forms

GAURA LINDHEIMERI 'CORRIES GOLD' Similar, but the leaves have yellow margins.

GAURA 'WHIRLING BUTTERFLIES' Profusely covered with whitish flowers and obvious red sepals.

Anemone x hybrida

Family: Ranunculaceae Common name: Japanese Anemone

This plant is of garden origin arising from the hybridising of *A. hupehensis* and *A. vitifolium*, both parents originating from the mountains of China, particularly the Himalayas.

The plant is generally sterile so will not produce seeds. Stems vary in height dependent upon the cultivar, up to 1.6m (5ft) tall. Basal leaves grow from a tufted rootstock having thin underground creeping stolons, from which the plant is propagated. Long leaf stalks, up to 30cm (12in) long carry three leaflets, each up to 10cm (4in) across, dark green and hairy beneath. Stems are purplish and flowers either pink or white with up to 11 tepals; all cultivars possess a distinctive central cluster of golden stamens. Prefers a moist humus-rich soil, it often flowers well in poorer soils. Position in full sun or light shade.

Varieties & Forms

ANEMONE 'HONORINE JOBERT' AGM A 19th-century hybrid with single white flowers, with up to nine tepals, approximately 6cm (3in) across.

ANEMONE 'HADSPEN ABUNDANCE' AGM Deep pink flowers with 6–9 tepals, growing up to 75cm (30in) tall.

ANEMONE 'KÖNIGIN' CHARLOTTE' AGM Has large deep-pink flowers and grows approximately 75cm (30in) tall.

Erica vagans 'Ida Britten'
Family: Ericaceae Common name: Cornish Heath

E vagans can be found in the wild in parts of France, Ireland and Cornwall, where it favours acidic soils, having a very restricted distribution along the Lizard peninsula. There are probably over 30 cultivars available.

A dwarf, evergreen, spreading shrub growing up to 40cm (16in) tall. Leaves are small, narrow and dark green, up to 1cm (½in) long, covering the thin wiry stems. Flowers form in late summer in dense racemes approximately 6cm (2½in) long. The pink flowers are small and bell shaped, up to about 5mm (¼in) long, and lasting for several weeks.

Grow in full sun in acid soil, which should be free draining. This species will tolerate neutral or slightly alkaline soils as well. Provides very good ground cover in sunny dry situations. Prune after flowering to remove all flowered stems with secateurs, or use shears if there are a lot of plants.

Varieties & Forms

ERICA VAGANS 'BIRCH GLOW' AGM Up to 30cm (12in) high with dark-pink flowers.

ERICA VAGANS 'LYONESSE' AGM Large clusters of small white flowers on compact plants, 25cm (10in) high.

Crinum x powellii AGM
Family: Amaryllidaceae

Produced by the hybridisation of two species originating from South Africa – *C. bulbispermum* and *C. moorei*.

Large bulbs produce strap-shaped leaves up to 1m (3ft) long; in mild winters the foliage persists throughout the year but otherwise the leaves die off so only the bulbs remain at ground level. Flower stems up to 1.2m (4ft) high are produced in late summer and early autumn; they are crowned with umbels of up to 12 large funnel-shaped pink flowers, approximately 12cm (5in) across.

Plant bulbs half buried at soil level in a warm, sunny, sheltered situation. Remove flowered stems as soon as the flowers fade and remove dying leaves to prevent disease, otherwise this plant is usually trouble free. Contact with the sap of this plant may irritate sensitive skin.

Varieties & Forms

CRINUM x POWELLII 'ALBUM'
Flowering profusely, having large white flowers.

Fuchsia 'Empress of Prussia'
Family: Onagraceae

Fuchsia magellanica arrived in the UK from South America in the late 18th century and has probably been one of several species used as the parents of many of the modern hybrids, because of its relative hardiness.

Of the 100 species originating from Central and South America, very few are hardy in the temperate climate of the British Isles, some tolerate mild winters but are often killed in the severe winters we experience approximately every 11 or 12 years.

This hybrid shown in the photograph, photographed at Wisley Gardens is permanently planted and in its sheltered position is able to remain for several years, however it is always worth while having one or two plants in pots with some winter protection to retain species or hybrids you may be particularly fond of. Growing to a height of approximately 90cm (3ft) it produces its foliage late in the season often not having leaves until late April.

Leaves are typical of many hybrids, a dull dark green, produced in opposite pairs, with a paler underside and about 6cm (2½in) long. Flowering over a long period the large pendulous flowers, dark red and carmine pink are approximately 7cm (3in) long flowering from July to the first frosts of October or November. Vine weevil may cause plant death, as they eat the roots.

Varieties & Forms

FUCHSIA 'DARK EYES' AGM Fairly hardy, red sepals and purplish double petals. Has a upright growth habit.

FUCHSIA 'CHILLERTON BEAUTY' Grows up to 1m (40in). Small flowers produced in large numbers, with dark-pink sepals and red petals.

Inula hookeri
Family: Asteraceae

This cheerful, herbaceous perennial plant is found growing wild in the Himalayas; its unusual ragged flowerheads liven up autumn borders.

Hairy stems growing up to 75cm (30in) carry hairy, toothed, light-green leaves, ovate or oblong, up to 15cm (6in) long. Pale yellow flowerheads approximately 8cm (3½in) across are produced in summer and autumn either singly or in clusters of two or three. These consist of bright yellow ray florets approximately 2.5cm (1in) long, and brownish yellow disc florets.

Grow in fertile and free-draining soil in full sun or partial shade.

Varieties & Forms

INULA ROYLEANA Pale orange flowerheads up to 12cm (5in) across on stems up to 60cm (24in) tall.

INULA MAGNIFICA Large golden-yellow flowerheads, up to 15cm (6in) across on stems up to 1.8m (6ft) tall.

Caryopteris x clandonensis
Family: Verbenaceae

A hybrid of garden origin therefore this particular species is not found in the wild; all wild species are however, found in eastern Asia.

A mound-forming deciduous shrub growing up to 1m (3ft) tall, flowering in late summer and autumn. Thin wiry stems grow in spring with toothed, lance-shaped, aromatic grey-green leaves up to 6cm (2½in) long. Pale, purplish-blue flowers are produced in the leaf axils; flowers are tubular with five lobes approximately 2.5cm (1in) long, with long prominent styles. Flowers form in tight clusters of up to 15 individual flowers, opening from pale-grey buds.

Grow in full sun in well-draining soil. Prune in spring, cutting growth back to a main branch network. Generally pest and disease free.

Varieties & Forms

CARYOPTERIS 'DARK KNIGHT' This plant has very grey foliage and very dark-blue flowers.

CARYOPTERIS 'WORCESTER GOLD' Has yellow leaves and pale-lilac flowers.

Calluna vulgaris 'Anne Marie' AGM

Family: Ericaceae Common name: Heather

C. vulgaris grows on heaths and moors in many parts of the UK and other European countries. There are several hundred forms and varieties, some found in the wild, others selected and cultivated by horticulturalists.

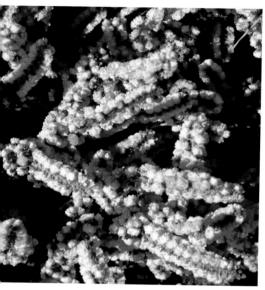

the winter. It will often thrive on soils that are less than fertile, being a good garden filler. Best when pruned annually after flowering using shears, making sure that all prunings are removed from the plant. Flowers and stems may be affected by botrytis during spells of wet weather, best treated by removal of badly infected growths, although sprays are available.

Varieties & Forms

CALLUNA VULGARIS 'KINLOCHRUEL' AGM Low growing with foliage turning bronze in winter and fully double pure-white flowers.

CALLUNA VULGARIS 'DARKNESS' AGM Only growing to 30cm (12in) one of the deepest red coloured flowers..

Typically of similar appearance to most *C. vulgaris* varieties. Flowering profusely during September and early October with small, dark-pink, fully double flowers at the ends of most stems. The plant grows to a height of 60cm (24in) if left unpruned. The wiry stems are covered with tiny evergreen scale-like leaves which crowd together along the stems.

Grow in full sun for maximum flowering in acid, well-draining soil but add plenty of organic material as an annual top dressing during

Cyclamen hederifolium AGM

Family: Primulaceae Common name: Sowbread

Originally from Mediterranean countries, this familiar plant has become naturalised in many other locations.

Growing from very large flattened tubers at or just below the soil surface, large clusters of heart-shaped leaves, appear in the late summer or early autumn following the flowering period. Leaves are dark green, spotted and streaked with silvery markings. The undersides of leaves and leaf petioles (stalks) are dark red, and they remain throughout the winter until June or July.

Leaves are up to 12cm (5in) long, often with very long petioles. Flowers grow to a height of approximately 12cm (5in) and open from the end of July until October with a peak period during early September. They are variable in shades of pink or white and up to 2cm (1in) long. Sometimes they have a sweet fragrance and are composed of five reflexed and twisted petals, with purplish red markings around the mouth formed by the petals. After flowering the flower stems twist into spirals to place the developing seed capsule just above the soil surface, remaining there until they split to release seeds in July.

Grow in shade, perhaps provided by deciduous trees; cyclamen prefer to be dry in the summer months but require a fertile humus-rich soil, so top dress regularly with

leaf mould or well-rotted garden compost after flowering. Slugs and snails may damage the young flowers and severe infestations of vine weevil may destroy the tubers.

Varieties & Forms

CYCLAMEN HEDERIFOLIUM 'ALBIFLORUM' Having pure-white flowers with no markings.

CYCLAMEN CILICIUM AGM A less vigorous plant producing flowers at the same time as leaves in autumn.

Colchicum speciosum

Family: Liliaceae Common name: Autumn Crocus

Originating from Eastern Europe, Turkey and the Caucasus mountains. The corms of this plant can be very large and some cultivars are very expensive.

This plant produces flowers from corms in the autumn before the leaves appear; the leaves are not produced until after the flowers have died. Because the large leaves persist until mid summer careful positioning is needed of this very beautiful plant.

Very attractive large flowers are goblet shaped on slender delicate tubes rising directly from the underground corm and growing up to 20cm (8in) high. Individual flowers are composed of six tepals, in varying shades of pink with deep golden-yellow anthers. Flowers can be easily damaged by wind or heavy rain.

Lance-shaped pleated, dark-green leaves, up to 25cm (10in) long, are produced after flowering on stems up to 40cm (16in) high.

Plant in summer 10cm (4in) deep in a sunny but sheltered position in fertile, free-draining soil as bulbs require dry conditions after leaves die down. Slugs may damage flowers and young foliage.

Varieties & Forms

COLCHICUM SPECIOSUM 'ALBUM'
Large white flowers which better resist adverse weather.

COLCHICUM 'WATERLILY' Each corm may produce up to five deep-pink flowers, fully double, up to 7 cm (3in).

Escallonia 'Iveyi' AGM
Family: Escalloniaceae

Believed to be a hybrid having as its parents *E. bifida* and *E. x exoniensis*, and to have originated at Caerhays Garden on the Cornish coast.

A vigorous evergreen shrub with stiff upright stems up to 3.2m (10ft) tall. Leaves are ovate, dark glossy green and up to 6cm (2½in) long. Flowers are produced from August through to early October in panicles up to 12cm (5in) long. The white flowers are fragrant, funnel-shaped and approximately 1cm (½in) across. The leaves may be lost in large numbers in frosty weather.

Grow in a fertile well-draining soil in full sun, sheltered from drying winds; does well against a sunny wall. Flowers form on previous years' growth and again on the current years' growth so pruning should be kept to a minimum, only remove very old stems to open the centre of the shrub.

Varieties & Forms

ESCALLONIA RUBRA Variable dark-pink or red flowers are produced in late summer and autumn.

ESCALLONIA RUBRA 'CRIMSON SPIRE' AGM Upright growing, has large crimson flowers, and is resistant to salt spray.

Aster 'Bahamas'

Family: Asteraceae Common name: Michaelmas Daisy

Belonging to a group of plants known as 'novi-belgii' although often only the variety name is shown in garden centres. Numerous hybrids have been raised over a period of 60 or 70 years and new varieties are introduced in an attempt to reduce the problems of wilt and mildew.

This plant will grow to a height of approximately 45cm (18in) and flowers in late summer and early autumn. Leaves are dark green and narrowly linear up to 10cm (4in) long on stems that are reddish green growing from rhizomatous rootstocks. Flowers are formed in corymbs over a long period – individual flower heads have bright-yellow disc florets and a row of magenta-red ray florets, up to 4cm (1½in) across.

Plant at the front of a border or in large containers in fertile soil in sun or light shade. Top dress and cut down after flowering to remove stems, which may get infected with mildew in certain conditions. Divide and replant after about three years. Slugs and snails may be a problem in wet springs and some damage may occur to young shoots.

Varieties & Forms

ASTER AMELLUS 'NOCTURNE' Deep lilac-blue flowers, growing to 75cm (30in) high.

ASTER 'ROYAL RUBY' Deep red double flowers, raised by Blooms of Bressingham.

Verbena bonariensis
Family: Verbenaceae

Originating from areas of damp open spaces in South America, including Argentina, Uruguay and Paraguay, verbena flowers in late summer and spreads by short rhizomes.

Upright stems grow quickly, attaining a height of 1.8m (6ft) if growing amongst other plants. The many-branched stems produce large numbers of flowers in cymes up to 5cm (2in) long, in summer and autumn. The bright purple flowers are salverform and approximately 6mm (¼in) across. Leaves are hairy, narrow and dark green with a purplish central vein, usually clasping the stem and up to 12cm (5in) long.

Grow in fertile, moist, but well-draining soil in full sun. Protect in severe winters with a thick mulch. Dry conditions may increase attacks of powdery mildew or aphids and leaf-hoppers.

Varieties & Forms

VERBENA HASTATA Probably the hardiest Verbena with purple, pink or white flowers, up to 1.4m (4ft) tall.

VERBENA RIGIDA AGM Has a tuberous rootstock, needing protection in very frosty conditions. Growing up to 70cm (28in) with purple or dark-red flowers.

Nerine bowdenii AGM
Family: Amaryllidaceae

Found in the wild in the Drakensberg Mountains of South Africa. It grows in rocky mountain screes in dry conditions and therefore requires a sunny position kept dry during the winter.

Flowers are produced in the autumn on stems emerging from the bare bulbs and quickly growing up to 50cm (18in) high. Umbels of flowers, approximately eight per stem, open from reddish bracts. The pink flowers are funnel shaped, composed of six recurving tepals, approximately 7cm (3in) across. As the flowers fade, narrow strap-shaped leaves up to 40cm (16in) long emerge from the bulbs.

Grow in a sheltered situation in full sun, in freely draining soil.

Planting at the base of a wall is often ideal. Bulbs should never be buried – plant on the surface with about half of the bulb exposed. Protect bulbs in frost-prone conditions.

Other species and cultivars are not frost-hardy and can only be grown in the milder south-western counties of England.

Abutilon megapotamicum AGM
Family: Malvaceae Common name: Trailing Abutilon

Originating from Brazil, this shrub is only hardy in the southern counties of the United Kingdom. Given the protection of a wall, it will survive most winters. As a precaution, take cuttings regularly and overwinter young plants under cover.

This is more or less an evergreen trailing shrub that will grow up to 1.8m (6ft) high with some support. It has thin green stems stretching out in many directions, carrying mid-green leaves which are ovate or heart shaped and up to 12cm (5in) long. In late summer and autumn, pendent flowers on long petioles are produced from the leaf axils. Flowers are approximately 4cm (1½in) long with folded yellow petals protruding from crimson calyces. When fully developed, flowers have a cluster of reddish purple stamens visible below the petals. In severe frosty weather the plant may loose most of its leaves.

Plant in a sheltered position in fertile, well-draining soil in full sun. A position against a south-facing house wall is often ideal. Whitefly and red spider mite may be a problem in dry weather.

Varieties & Forms

ABUTILON MEGAPOTAMICUM 'VARIEGATUM' Golden-yellow blotches appear on the leaves, more obvious on younger leaves.

Gentiana scabra

Family: Gentianiaceae Common name: Japanese Gentian

Originating from Japan and other Northern Asian countries this plant can be found growing on woodland edges often in damp soils.

Leaves are produced in pairs, are dark green, narrow and pointed up to 4cm (1½in) long. Usually evergreen, in cold winters the plant can lose most of its leaves.

Grow in moisture-retentive soil, but plants benefit from a top dressing of grit to lessen fungal disease attacks. Gentians can be grown in sun or partial shade but avoid a situation where overhanging tree branches drip excessively on to flowers and plant leaves. Flowers can be affected by botrytis, so remove any decaying flowers or stems, which can be particularly prevalent during damp autumn weather.

Plants grow up to 25cm (10in) high and produce clusters of blue flowers at the tips of the stems over a long period during September to November, dependent upon weather conditions. Flowers are tubular, approximately 2.5cm (1in) long, with slightly spreading lobes when fully open. The petals are dark blue with lighter blue stripes and splashes.

Varieties & Forms

GENTIANA SINO-ORNATA AGM
Short growing mat-forming plants with striped dark-blue flowers.

GENTIANA ASCLEPIADEA AGM
A taller-growing plant with numerous dark-blue tubular flowers.

Schizostylis coccinea

Family: Iridaceae Common name: Kaffir Lily

Growing wild in damp meadows and alongside rivers and streams in South Africa, this plant develops from underground rhizomes.

Flowering stems are produced from late summer to early winter, and grow to 60cm (24in) high. Spikes of up to 12 flowers remain open for long periods. Bright scarlet flowers are salverform consisting of six petals and a long tube approximately 3.5cm (1½in) across. Leaves are sword-shaped, up to 40cm (16in) high and generally basal, although occasionally they appear on the flowering stems.

Grow in full sun in a moisture-retentive soil. Top dress regularly with well-rotted garden compost.

Split crowded clumps every few years for new vigorous growth.

Varieties & Forms

SCHIZOSTYLIS COCCINEA 'MAJOR' AGM Has larger flowers produced in greater abundance than other varieties.

SCHIZOSTYLIS COCCINEA VAR. ALBA AGM White flowers tinged with pink.

SCHIZOSTYLIS COCCINEA 'JENNIFER' AGM Large pink flowers.

Lavatera thuringiaca 'Rosea' AGM
Family: Malvaceae Common name: Tree Lavatera

Originally from Eastern European countries, but now there are many selections and hybrids. Approximately ten named cultivars exist but only two or three are generally available.

As the common name suggests this plant will quickly grow to a height of 3m (10ft) but it is short lived and rarely survives for more than 10 years. Upright stems remain green and are covered in short hairs as are the three lobed leaves up to 10cm (4in) long, which have a dull greyish appearance and long petioles. Leaves are usually shed during cold weather but a mild winter will result in the shrub retaining the leaves throughout the winter until new leaves form in spring. Flowers form in summer and continue over a long period often until the first frosts. Individual flowers are bright pink, funnel shaped up to 8cm (3½in) across with scalloped petals. They are produced in axillary racemes, early in the season but often singly as the season progresses.

The shrub is susceptible to 'wind rock' and very frosty conditions, which can terminate an apparently healthy plant. Grow in fertile soil in full sun, protected from cold drying winds. Prune in spring ensuring that no frosts are imminent, removing all growth back to a main branch framework.

Osteospermum jucundum AGM
Family: Asteraceae

Originating from South Africa, this is really the only truly hardy osteospermum. Numerous osteospermum hybrids are available for seasonal bedding displays, but most will not survive frosts.

This plant spreads by rhizomes growing over the soil surface and forming large evergreen clumps that will cover quite large areas in ideal growing conditions. Leaves grow up to 10cm (4in) long, are variable, narrow and linear, grey-green in colour, hairy and feel sticky.

Flowers are produced over a long period, often throughout the year with suitable conditions. Usually there are two main flushes, in the spring and again in the autumn. Flowers form on long stems that hold them clear of the foliage. They are variable in colour, from almost white to pinkish-purple, in ray florets with contrasting disc florets usually of a dark purple, opening to yellow as the stamens develop. The flowerheads are up to 6cm (2½in) in diameter.

Grow in a sunny position but sheltered from cold winds in a well-draining soil. This plant often does best when in the shelter of a wall or hedge. Keep the roots moist in the summer but dry in the winter.

Crocus speciosus AGM

Family: Iridaceae Common name: Autumn Crocus

This crocus is originally from Turkey and other countries of the Caucasus Mountains, as far north as Ukraine and east to Iran.

In October or November solitary flowers are produced from each corm, growing quickly to a height of 10cm (4in). Long pale-blue tubes are topped with six light-blue tepals with deep-blue veins. The central flowerparts of stamens and a much-divided style are golden-yellow. Although there is some leaf growth after flowering, the leaves often do not grow until the spring, when they reach 15cm (6in) tall.

The delicate flowers can be damaged by winds, so plant in a sheltered situation in full sun or light shade. They can also be naturalised in lawns where the grass foliage provides some shelter.

Colonies develop quickly from offsets and seed so dig up and divide every few years in spring, before the foliage disappears.

Varieties & Forms

CROCUS SPECIOSUS FORM ALBUM AGM Has beautiful pure white flowers with golden anthers and style.

CROCUS SPECIOSUS 'CONQUEROR' Has strong erect flowers with a deep-blue colour.

Phygelius x rectus 'Yapor'
Family Scrophulariacae

This is a hybrid of two species found growing wild in South Africa and has as one of its parents *P. capensis*, known as the Cape Figwort. Numerous named hybrid varieties have been raised over the last 20 years.

The shrub is upright growing and may reach 1.5m (5ft) in a good sheltered position, although it is susceptible to frost damage, which may reduce its ultimate height. Suckers naturally occur from below ground level, so its spread may indeed be greater than its height.

Leaves are ovate, light green and up to 10cm (4in) long. Loose panicles, up to 20cm (8in), of orange-red flowers are produced at the end of new growths or on short lateral branches arising on older stems. Individual flowers are tubular, often with a distinct curve and up to 5cm (2in) long.

A tender shrub which may be badly damaged in very cold frosty winters, resulting in a need to prune almost down to ground level. Position in full sun or light shade – does well at the base of a house wall – and provide a fertile well draining soil.

Varieties & Forms

PHYGELIUS X RECTUS 'MOONRAKER' Grows up to 1m (40in) producing pale-yellow flowers during late summer and autumn.

PHYGELIUS X RECTUS 'DEVIL'S TEARS' Has dark-red flowers with a paler throat.

Fuchsia 'Genii' AGM
Family: Onagraceae

This low-growing deciduous tender shrub is of garden origin. There are several thousand fuchsia cultivars and their origin is often unclear, as they have been hybridised for many years.

Mulch in autumn to protect the rootstock. In very cold winters, all growth above ground will be killed, but the plant will regrow from buds below ground level. The only really reliable hardy fuchsia is *F. magellanica*.

Varieties & Forms

FUCHSIA MAGELLANICA 'VARIEGATA' Leaves have cream margins and typical red and purple flowers.

FUCHSIA MAGELLANICA var MOLINAE Reportedly the hardiest fuchsia, having green stems and leaves, and pale-pink flowers.

FUCHSIA 'MME CORNELLISSEN' Vigorous, growing up to 1m (40in) with red and pinkish-white flowers.

Low growing, – up to 80cm (32in) high – young shoots are red and the young leaves are lime green, turning darker green as they age. Leaves are ovate, up to 7cm (3in) long, persisting throughout the year if the winter is mild. Flowers produced in late summer and autumn have a cerise calyx and a violet-blue corolla fading to purplish red. They are approximately 3cm (1¼in) long with a longer style and are often followed by shiny black fruits up to 1cm (½in) across.

Plant in full sun in well-draining fertile soil. Prune in spring as low as required to obvious new buds.

Lonicera japonica

Family: Caprifoliaceae Common name: Japanese Honeysuckle

Found in the wild in China, Taiwan, Korea and Japan and naturalised in parts of the USA, where it flowers in July and August.

A vigorous, more or less evergreen twining shrub, scrambling up supports or other plants to approximately 8m (25ft). Leaves are generally ovate, light-green and up to 7cm (3in) long.

Flowers form in the leaf axils over a long flowering period, commencing in late spring, continuing spasmodically through the summer and with a final fling in the autumn. Flowers are white, fragrant and two lipped, up to 3cm (1¼in) long, fading to yellow as they age, giving an attractive two

tone effect. Sometimes small ovoid blackish fruits are produced after the flowers.

Grows well in most soils, in light shade. Prune in spring to keep long growths under control or it can become a tangled thicket.

Varieties & Forms

LONICERA JAPONICA 'AUREORETICULATA' Has leaves with yellow veins, not as vigorous and produces fewer flowers.

LONICERA JAPONICA 'HALLIANA' AGM Very vigorous, having slightly larger flowers than other varieties.

LONICERA JAPONICA 'SUPERBA' Smaller leaves and scarlet flowers up to 5cm (2in) long.

Passiflora caerulea AGM

Family: Passifloraceae Common name: Blue passion flower

Originating from South American countries, this climbing plant is hardy in most areas, except in very cold frosty winters, when it may be killed down to ground level.

flowering plant. Ten tepals with a corona of fleshy filaments surround the stamens and a triple style. Overall, flowers are up to 10cm (4in) across but are very short lived, falling quickly if not pollinated. Those that are pollinated are followed by ovoid green fruits turning yellow as they ripen. Fruits are edible but rather tasteless with very little flesh surrounding the dark, blackish seeds.

Position in full sun, with some protection from cold drying winds. Red spider mite or whitefly may be a problem in dry conditions, which also causes flowers to fall prematurely.

This climber will grow rapidly and cover its allotted space very quickly. The thin wiry stems are brittle and carry five lobed dark-green leaves and many tendrils, which rapidly coil to support the stems that often manage to grow 6–7m (around 20ft) in a season.

From mid summer to late autumn flowers are produced along the new stems or from short growths from older wood. Flowers are pale blue with a central ring of purplish filaments and one of the most unusual flower formation of any

Varieties & Forms

PASSIFLORA 'AMETHYST' AGM
Has pale violet-purple flowers up to 12cm (5in) across.

PASSIFLORA 'CONSTANCE ELLIOTT' Large white fragrant flowers with pale blue contrasting filaments.

Elaeagnus macrophylla
Family: Elaeagnaceae

Originally found growing on the islands of Japan often in coastal woodlands so it is a useful evergreen shrub for exposed areas where salt spray, which can damage some evergreen plants, is a problem.

An attractive evergreen shrub growing up to 2m (6ft). It has glossy dark-green leaves, which are ovate and up to 8cm (3in) long with a silvery mealy underside. Young stems are attractively light brown and scaly.

Flowers generally open in late autumn or early winter and are small and inconspicuous but have a delightful fragrance. Borne in small axillary clusters, they are tubular with splayed mouths, silvery white in colour and up to 2cm (1in) long. Sometimes after flowering, small ovoid fruits with unusual striped markings are produced up to 2cm (1in) long. Grow in fertile soil in full sun or light shade.

Varieties & Forms

ELAEAGNUS X EBBINGII Probably a hybrid between *E.pungens* and *E. macrophylla*, similar habit but flowering in late winter or early spring.

ELAEAGNUS 'GILT EDGE' AGM Has dark-green leaves edged with cream and grey.

Liriope muscari AGM
Family: Liliaceae Common name: Lilyturf

Found in the wild growing on woodland edges in China, Japan and other Far Eastern countries when it flowers in late summer and autumn.

The plant forms compact tufts of dark-green, linear, grass-like leaves up to 40cm (16in) high. During October and November dense spikes of small purplish flowers are produced on reddish green stems up to 30cm (12in) tall. Flower stems may be flattened and up to 2.5cm (1in) wide. Sometimes the flowers are followed by the formation of black seeds.

Grow in moderately fertile soil with a good supply of organic matter, ensuring that the soil is not wet or waterlogged. Select a shaded or lightly shaded position and protect from cold drying winds. The plant is usually pest and disease free although slugs and snails may damage young shoots and flower stems.

Varieties & Forms

LIRIOPE MUSCARI 'JOHN BURCH'
Has golden variegated leaves and slightly larger flowers.

LIRIOPE MUSCARI 'MONROE WHITE' Has many stems of white flowers and does best in full shade.

Convolvulus cneorum AGM
Family: Convolvulaceae

Many species of bindweed are climbing plants but this plant, originating from Mediterranean countries, is a rather tender compact shrub.

Growing to a height of 60cm (24in) the plant tends to be very bushy but compact. Leaves are narrow and hairy, having a silver appearance, and up to 6cm (2½in) long. Flower buds are pink, produced in clusters in the leaf axils, and open to display showy white flowers up to 5cm (2in) across, with deep-yellow centres and yellow markings. Flowering commences in late spring and continues spasmodically throughout summer and autumn.

Grow in well-drained soil in a sunny position; dead-head regularly and trim in late spring to retain shape and remove any dead shoots or very congested growth.

Varieties & Forms

CONVOLVULUS BOISSIERI
Creeping, mat-forming plant with silver-grey leaves and white flowers with yellow centres.

CONVOLVULUS SABATIUS AGM
Only hardy in the milder counties of the UK. A trailing perennial with blue flowers over a long period.

Fatsia japonica AGM

Family: Araliaceae Common name: Japanese Aralia

An evergreen shrub originating from Korea and Japan where it grows in shaded positions on woodland edges. Grown mainly for its highly decorative large evergreen leaves.

Upright, stiff stems grow quickly, often reaching a height of 3.5m (11ft). Very large palmately lobed leaves are dark green and shiny with 7 to 10 lobes on petioles up to 40cm (16in) long. In late autumn, large open, compound umbels of numerous creamy white flowers form up to 40cm (16in) across. The unusual flowers appear to be spiky due to the small petals and prominent stamens. The leaves are popular in floral displays.

Grows well in shady conditions although flowering is reduced if in dense shade. Growing points may be damaged in hard winters when temperatures fall below −10°C.

Other forms of *F.japonica* are not fully hardy so are not included here.

Osmanthus x fortunei

Family: Oleaceae

Of garden origin, formed by the hybridisation between *O. fragrans* and *O. heterophyllus* and has inherited some qualities from both parents.

This evergreen shrub grows to 4m (13ft) and has variable, dark-green, leathery leaves some with spiny toothed margins. These leaves are up to 8cm (3½in) long. Very fragrant tubular white flowers are produced in the leaf axils during September to November. Clusters of up to 12 flowers open over a long period: the tube is up to 3cm (1¼in) long and opens to 1cm (½in) across.

Grow in semi-shade, on fertile, freely draining but moist soil with adequate supplies of organic material. Shelter from cold drying winds. Pruning is only necessary to retain shape and to keep within its allotted space.

Varieties & Forms

OSMANTHUS x FORTUNEI 'SAN JOSE' The leaves are narrower and carry more spines.

Verbena 'Seabrook's Lavender'

Family: Verbenaceae

Many Verbena cultivars grown in our gardens are treated as annuals and provide long-lasting, colourful displays during the summer months in beds, borders, pots and tubs. However some species will tolerate temperatures as low as -10C.

This cultivar is useful as a short-lived perennial, surviving most winters. Growing to a height of 40cm (18in) with a similar spread, the plant produces flowers over a long period of months. The slightly fragrant flowers grow in dense flower heads up to 5cm (2in) across composed of lavender-blue salverform flowers. Tubular corollas approximately 1cm (½in) long open at the mouth with five corolla lobes. The plant is somewhat hairy overall and the dark-green, toothed leaves are produced in opposite pairs, up to 8cm (3in) long.

The plant will tolerate a wide variety of soil types, but prefers a moisture retentive soil in full sun or light shade. Prune regularly during the growing season to keep tidy and to lengthen the flowering period. Powdery mildew may be a problem in wet seasons and capsids and leafhoppers may damage the growing points, reducing flowering.

Varieties & Forms

VERBENA 'SISSINGHURST' AGM

Only growing to a height of 30cm (12in) this cultivar has dark pink flowers.

VERBENA 'SILVER ANNE' AGM

Sweetly scented light pink flowers that fade to white, producing a two-tone effect.

Hebe 'Autumn Glory'
Family: Scrophulariaceae

A hybrid raised over 100 years ago, believed to have
H. pimeloides and *H. x franciscana* as its parents. A useful evergreen hebe which may have flowers open for several months.

A small compact evergreen shrub,
usually attaining a height of 75cm
(30in), although in a sheltered
position it may grow taller. The
small, narrow ovate leaves are
glossy purplish-green, up to 5cm
(2in) long. The purplish foliage
is often more conspicuous in the
colder winter months.

Small racemes of flowers form
in the autumn and open slowly
throughout October to December.
The flower heads, up to 3cm (1¼in)
long, are composed of many small
deep-purple flowers. Grow in full
sun, preferably sheltered from cold
drying winds and in a fertile but
well-draining soil.

Varieties & Forms

**HEBE X FRANCISCANA
'VARIEGATA' AGM**
Has violet-blue flower spikes and creamy
white margined leaves.

HEBE 'GREAT ORME' AGM Glossy
dark-green leaves, reddish stems and
dark-pink flowers in spikes up to 8cm
(3in) long.

Solanum jasminoides
Family: Solanaceae Common name: Potato Vine

Belonging to a large family of plants, including the potato and aubergine, surprisingly many species are poisonous. *S. jasminoides* originates from South America.

A trailing, scrambling plant with narrow lance shaped dark-green leaves up to 5cm (2in) long. In late summer and autumn flowers form in the leaf axils and in terminal clusters of up to 15 flowers. The off-white flowers are star shaped, fragrant and up to 3cm (1¼in) across. Grow in fertile, well-draining soil, neutral to alkaline is best. Shelter from cold drying winds. As the plant is not self supporting tie in extension growths regularly. Prune in spring, shortening long growths and cut back shorter flowered stems to three or four buds.

Varieties

SOLANUM JASMINOIDES 'ALBUM' AGM Has pure white flowers.

SOLANUM CRISPUM 'GLASNEVIN' AGM Purplish-blue flowers appear in great profusion; needs to be grown in a sheltered position.

EARLY
WINTER

It is a delight to see flowers as the days shorten and the weather cools, and many of the chosen plants here provide fragrance for the winter garden.

Weeks 49-52

Jasminum nudiflorum AGM

Family: Apocynaceae Common name: Winter flowering jasmine

One of many jasmines, *J. nudiflorum* was introduced in 1844 by avid plant hunters to China and other Asian countries. It may be trained against a fence or a wall or allowed to scramble through other shrubs so that the yellow flowers can brighten up the dark winter months. Its scientific name translates as 'naked flowers', this of course relates to the plant flowering during the winter months, when there are no leaves on the plant.

A deciduous straggling shrub (some plants are tidier than others) growing up to 3.5m (12ft) in all directions unless pruned to keep it within its allotted space. Long arching stems bear opposite pinnate, dark green leaves. The leaf is divided into three leaflets approximately 4cm (1½in) long.

Flowers are produced over a long period, often starting in November and continuing through favourable weather conditions until March or early April. Bright-yellow flowers are up to 2cm (1in) across and salverform. Buds are conspicuously tinged with red and emerge from large-scale leaves, which enclose the bud. Unfortunately, the flowers of this jasmine do not have a fragrance; leaves follow after flowering, usually in April.

Position shrubs in fertile well-draining soil in full sun to maximise flowering. Prune each year when established by removing long untidy stems and older shoots once flowering is finished.

Viburnum x bodnantense 'Dawn' AGM
Family: Caprifoliaceae

A hybrid produced by a natural cross of *V. farreri* and *V. grandiflorum*. It takes its specific name from the famous Bodnant garden in North Wales, from where it originated.

A deciduous shrub with reddish stems up to 2.5m (7ft) high, with a spread of 2m (6ft). Produces strongly fragranced, tubular, pale-pink flowers in clusters over several months. Individual flowers are up to 1cm (½in) across in clusters up to 6–7cm (1½–2in) in diameter, commencing in November and then flowering spasmodically until late March.

Leaves are produced after flowering, deep green with prominent sunken veins and red leaf stalks. They are approximately 7.5–9cm (3in–4in) long and 3.5–5cm (1½in–2in) wide, arranged in opposite pairs sparsely along the branches. Sometimes the new leaves are flushed red and in the autumn some leaves exhibit red or orange shades.

Grow in fertile soil that is rich in organic matter in light shade. It will tolerate a sunny position but the flowers may be damaged by early-morning frosts.

Varieties & Forms

VIBURNUM x BODNANTENSE 'CHARLES LAMONT' AGM With rich-pink, slightly larger flowers.

VIBURNUM x BODNANTENSE 'DEBEN' AGM Has white flowers, with light-pink tinges.

Mahonia x media 'Buckland' AGM
Family: Berberidaceae

This hybrid, one of several, is formed by the hybridisation between *M. japonica* and *M. lomariifolia*; there are many named selections which are difficult to tell apart.

The plant will ultimately grow to a large size, sometimes to 4m (13ft) tall after many years, so is suitable only for large gardens. Upright, stiff branches bear large evergreen pinnate leaves up to 45cm (18in) long composed of glossy greyish-green leaflets with spiny toothed margins. Flowers are produced from the end of October to early December with long racemes, up to 45cm (18in) long, composed of numerous dull yellow, slightly fragrant flowers.

Grow in light shade for maximum flowering; the plant will withstand heavier shade but with a consequent loss of flowering.

A moist soil is best with a good supply of organic material, but it will not tolerate boggy or very wet soils in winter. Generally found to be pest and disease free. Prune only to remove weak or old stems and to shape the plant to fit its allocated space.

Varieties & Forms

MAHONIA x MEDIA 'CHARITY' AGM This plant originated at Savill Gardens in Windsor Great Park and the original plant can still be seen to this day. It is a hybrid between *M. japonica* and *M. media*.

Camellia sasanqua

Family: Ericaceae

An autumn-flowering camellia that originates from Japan, it is useful for extending the season of the more commonly grown *C.japonica*.

This shrub is evergreen and quite vigorous, growing up to 3m (10ft). Glossy dark-green leaves up to 8cm (3in) long with a paler underside provide a year-round attractive appearance.

Large flower buds appear during the summer and open during mild weather conditions in autumn and early winter. Fragrant white flowers have six petals and are cup-shaped, up to 8cm (3in) across with a prominent central cluster of yellow stamens.

This camellia requires an acid soil, and some shade, although it will tolerate a sunny site. However avoid a position where early-morning sun can damage flowers during very frosty weather. Roots should not be allowed to dry out so top dress regularly with well-rotted garden compost or other organic material in order that that the rooting area is kept cool.

Varieties & Forms

CAMELLLIA SASANQUA 'SHISHIGASHIRA' Has semi-double dark-pink flowers.

CAMELLIA SASANQUA 'COTTON CANDY' Light-pink double flowers are produced throughout the autumn.

Iris unguicularis 'Walter Butt'
Family: Iridaceae

I. unguicularis originates from North Africa and eastern Mediterranean countries including Turkey and Greece, growing on well-drained rocky hillsides.

The plant forms thick rhizomatous clumps of light-green leaves growing up to 70cm (28in) tall. Flowers are violet-blue, fragrant and often hidden away in the untidy foliage. Flowers are up to 10cm (4in) across with white and yellow markings on the fall petals and produced from December, although the main flowering period is in March. Mild winter weather can encourage flowering at any time.

Most clones of this iris are infected with virus that spoils the foliage, killing off leaf tips and browning the leaf margins, which dry and make the plant look untidy. Carefully remove these affected leaves regularly to improve the plant's appearance, particularly during the flowering period.

Plant in well-drained soil in a sunny position; often plants do best at the base of a wall or hedge.

Varieties & Forms

IRIS UNGUICULARIS 'MARY BARNARD' Produces deep-blue almost purple flowers in late winter/early spring.

IRIS UNGUICULARIS 'ALBA' Has white flowers with a distinct yellow stripe. Flowers of this form may be damaged by hard frosts.

Prunus x subhirtella 'Autumnalis Rosea' AGM

Family: Rosaceae Common name: Rosebud Cherry

This hybrid cherry has *P. incisa* and *P. pendula* as its parents, the original coming from Japan, but there are many varieties and selections.

A small-spreading tree if grown with a trunk, or a large shrub, reaching a height of 8m (25ft) although as it is slow growing it takes many years to reach this size.

Flowers are produced intermittently depending upon weather conditions from October to March. They form in clusters of up to five, are semi-double pinkish-white and up to 2cm (¾in) across. Ovate leaves form after flowering, bronze at first, turning dark green later, with toothed margins up to 8cm (3in) long. Sometimes the leaves turn yellowish or orange in the autumn.

As the tree habit is slightly spreading, allow plenty of room when deciding where to plant this cherry. Minimal pruning is needed to remove dead or crossing stems to maintain an open habit. As with all cherry trees, this one is susceptible to the usual infections of silver leaf disease and blossom wilt. Pruning should therefore be carried out in summer, when there is less possibility of fungal infection.

Varieties & Forms

PRUNUS SUBHIRTELLA 'AUTUMNALIS' AGM This small tree is very similar but has fewer flowers that are paler, almost white.

Viburnum tinus

Family: Caprifoliaceae
Common name: Laurustinus

Originating from Mediterranean areas, the plant is at home in most parts of the United Kingdom. In the south-east it will sometimes commence to flower in September and continue until April. But that is not the end of its interest, as in some years the flowers are succeeded by blue/black berries and, being evergreen, there is always the foliage to look at.

Evergreen large shrub, up to 4m (13ft) with a spread of up to 2m (6ft). Leaves are leathery and tough, oval or oblong in shape and up to 10cm (4in) long, opposite and usually with a red petiole. This shrub, although evergreen, has a habit of shedding leaves throughout the summer and autumn. Unfortunately, an unpleasant aroma is produced when the foliage is wet.

Flowers are produced in umbels 10cm (4in) across from October to April. Individual flowers, commencing with pink buds and opening to pale-pink or off-white, are approximately 1cm (½in) across, some clones having a delicate fragrance in sunny dry conditions. The leaves can be severely damaged by attacks from the viburnum beetle, for which there is no recommended pesticide to control infestations.

Varieties & Forms

Although there are many species and varieties of viburnum, only a few flower during the winter months.

'EVE PRICE' AGM Usually the form available in most garden centres, this has dark-pink flower buds.

'GWENLLIAN' AGM Dark-pink flower buds, and produces blue-black fruits freely.

'LUCIDUM' Slightly larger flowers and very shiny dark-green leaves.

'VARIEGATUM' Has creamy/yellow leaf margins, not as hardy as others and may occasionally be damaged by frosts.

Helleborus niger AGM

Family: Ranunculaceae Common name: Christmas rose

Found in many European countries including Germany, Austria and Italy. The specific name 'niger' meaning black relates to the black fleshy roots.

A fleshy rooted, clump-forming perennial with long-lasting leaves. New leaves are produced after flowering and the dark-green leathery leaves stay on the plant over winter. Leaves are palmate with 7–9 leaflets, each oblong and 12–20cm (5-8in), sometimes toothed towards the tip.

Flower stems arise from the crown of the plant and are purplish-green, growing to a height of 30cm (12in). They produce saucer-shaped flowers up to 7cm (3in) across. Pure white waxy flowers, up to three per stem have greenish centres and clusters of creamy-yellow stamens. Sometimes petals are marked with pink on the outside, obvious only before the flowers open.

All prefer a moisture-retentive soil with plenty of humus in neutral or slightly alkaline conditions. Light shade is tolerated but dense shade will reduce the number of flowers produced. There are numerous named hybrids and selected forms, two of which are listed below.

Varieties & Forms

HELLEBORUS NIGER Subsp MACRANTHUS Slightly larger flowers up to 11cm (4in) across and spiny-toothed, bluish-tinged dark-green leaves.

HELLEBORUS NIGER 'POTTER'S WHEEL' Large saucer-shaped flowers, green centres. Flowers fade to pink.

Erica x darleyensis 'Archie Graham'

Family: Ericaceae Common name: Darley Dale Heath

There are numerous named hybrids of the form *Erica x darleyensis* formed by the crossing of *Erica carnea* and *Erica erigena*, most of them flowering during the winter months.

Leaves are small, up to 12mm (½in) long and bright green, appearing to be in whorls around the slender wiry stems. Plants grow to a height of approximately 50cm (20in) and can form a wide spreading plant up to 75cm (30in) across.

Flowers are produced in racemes 10–15cm (4–6in) long over a very long flowering period. Individual flowers are pink and urn-shaped, and darken as they age. Dark chocolate-coloured stamens project from the mouths. Prune in spring after flowering, ensuring all prunings are removed.

Varieties & Forms

ERICA x D. 'KRAMER'S ROTE' AGM
A fairly vigorous selection with large red flowers.

ERICA x D. 'WHITE GLOW' Has a compact growth habit, covered in pure-white flowers, with dark-coloured anthers.

ERICA x D. 'SILBERSCHMELZE'
Often grown under a variety of other names, having white flowers and leaves that change from cream to dark-green to reddish as the seasons change.

Lonicera x purpusii 'Winter Beauty' AGM
Family: Caprifoliaceae

This hybrid 'Honeysuckle' of garden origin is shrubby and not a climber. This shrub flowers spasmodically throughout the winter, sometimes starting in November, but usually at its peak at the end of February or early March. Even in the coldest winter weather flowers can be seen.

White fragrant flowers with prominent golden yellow stamens up to 4cm (1½in) are produced in clusters on bare leafless stems. After flowering in spring, light-green ovate leaves up to 7.5cm (3in) in pairs are produced. They turn a darker green as the season advances. The shrub will grow to 2m (6ft) with a spread of 2.5m (8ft). Although not a climbing plant the shrub can be pruned to a shape against a wall or fence.

Prune in spring after flowering to remove a few older branches and crossing, intertwining or non-flowering shoots.

Varieties & Forms

LONICERA STANDISHII White fragrant flowers, produced from winter to early spring.

LONICERA FRAGRANTISSIMA Similar to 'Winter Beauty' but this is more vigorous having slightly smaller creamy-white flowers. Red berries form after flowering.

Clematis cirrhosa

Family: Ranunculaceae

Originates from the Balearic islands, growing in the mountains and scrambling over rocks and other shrubs.

An evergreen climbing plant growing up to 3.5m (11ft) with thin wiry clinging stems. Opposite leaves are fern-like, light green with bronzing undersides. As with most climbing clematis, the leaves are used as tendrils to support the stems. Flowers are produced over a long period of time during the winter months, sometimes even into March. These are bell-shaped with four petals, creamy yellow, often flecked inside with dark red and are produced in clusters of four or five. Following flowering, decorative silver feathery seed heads are seen for several weeks.

Remove dead, weak or diseased stems immediately after flowering to tidy the plant and keep it within bounds. It is important to carry out the pruning immediately after flowering, as flowers are produced on previous year's growth.

Cool moisture-retentive soils are preferred, but ensure that it is freely draining. The best position is against a sheltered wall or fence. It is used to advantage when it is allowed to clamber through a deciduous shrub such as a rose.

Varieties & Forms

CLEMATIS CIRRHOSA Var. BALEARICA Similar but the flowers are fragrant and have red streaking inside the petals.

CLEMATIS CIRRHOSA 'FRECKLES' AGM Has cream-coloured flowers with heavy spotting and streaks of red.

Mahonia lomariifolia AGM

Family: Berberidaceae

Found in the wild in the Himalayan Mountains in Yunnan and Northern Burma. A very large shrub that may attain almost tree-like size in the wild, growing up to 10m (33ft).

In cultivation this shrub generally grows to a maximum height of 4m (13ft). Stems are yellowish-grey and prominently ringed where old leaves have died.

Leaves are evergreen and up to 75cm (30in) long with up to 18 pairs of leathery dark-green leaflets, having sharply pointed margins. Flowers are yellow and produced in terminal erect racemes from October to December. Grow in a sheltered location to protect from cold, drying winds.

Although it has been known in cultivation since 1931, there are no selected varieties. It is, however, one of the parents of *M x media* 'Charity' (see Varieties & Forms, plant 147).

Index

A

Abelia x grandiflora 120
Abutilon megapotamicum 143
Acacia dealbata 15
Allium karataviense 85
Alstroemeria psittacina 112
Amelanchier lamarckii 57
Anemone blanda 50
Anemone nemerosa 54
Anemone x hybrida 130
Arbutus unedo 128
Aster 'Bahamas' 140
Astrantia maxima 97
Aubrieta cultorum 43

B

Berberis darwinii 65
Bergenia 'Silberlicht' 30
Brachyglottis laxifolia 100
Buddleja alternifolia 86
Buddleja globosa 92

C

Calluna vulgaris 'Anne Marie' 136
Caltha palustris 59
Camellia japonica 14
Camellia sasanqua 165
Campanula lactiflora 72
Campsis grandiflora 122
Caryopteris x clandonensis 135
Ceratostigma willmottianum 116
Chaenomeles speciosa 'Etna' 51 60
Chimonanthus praecox 10
Chionodoxa forbesii 48
Choisya ternata 71
Clematis alpina 90
Clematis cirrhosa 172
Clematis montana 'Rubens 69
Clematis tangutica 125
Colchicum speciosum 138
Covolvulus cneorum 155
Corylopsis pauciflora 41
Crocosmia 'Lucifer' 101
Crinum x powellii 132
Crocus speciosus 148
Crocus tommasinianus 17
Cyclamen coum 13

Cyclamen hederifolium 137 153
Cytisus x praecox 68

D

Daphne mezereum 'Bowles Variety' 36
Daphne odora 'Aureomarginata' 21
Deutzia longifolia 'Veitchii' 95

E

Echinacea purpurea 103
Elaeagnus x ebbingii 153
Erica arborea 'Alpina' 61
Erica erigena 23
Erica lusitanica 16
Erica carnea 'C J Backhouse' 27
Erica 'Springwood White' 29
Erica vagans 'Ida Britten' 131
Eranthis hyemalis 24
Erigeron glaucus 'Elstead Pink' 94 105
Erythronium americanum 66
Escallonia 'Apple Blossom' 82
Escallonia ' Iveyi' 139
Eucomis 'Sparkling Burgundy' 119
Eucryphia glutinosa 116
Euphorbia polychroma 67

F

Fatsia japonica 156
Forsythia x intermedia 'Spectabilis' 33
Fuchsia genii 150
Fuchsia 'Empress of Prussia' 133

G

Galanthus nivalis 19
Galtonia candicans 117
Gaura lindheimeri 129
Garrya elliptica 25
Genista lydia 74
Gentiana scabra 144
Geranium pratense 'Plenum Violaceum' 107
Geranium sanguineum 70

H

Hamamelis mollis 12
Hebe 'Autumn Glory' 160
Hebe salicifolia 106
Helianthus x multiflorus 109

Published in 2014 by Albury Books
Albury Court, Albury, Thame,
Oxfordshire, OX9 2LP
www.alburybooks.com

Designed by Creative Plus Publishing Limited
151 High Street
Billericay
Essex CM12 9AB
www.creative-plus.co.uk

A CIP catalogue record is available from the British Libriary

Printed in Spain by Imago
ISBN 13: 978-1-910235-29-4